# CANICROSS

## FOR FUN AND FITNESS



Emily Thomas

THE CROWOOD PRESS

# CONTENTS

# FOREWORD

I first came across canisports in 2006 and took part in my first canicross 'race' with my two cocker spaniels in 2007. It really was experimental for me and truthfully, I barely knew what I was doing, beyond making sure my dogs were physically capable of running 5km (3mi) attached to me – a very poor excuse for a runner.

I look back at photos of our kit then and smile – I was wearing a big, baggy T-shirt and jogging bottoms. My spaniels wore their fleece-lined, short walking harnesses and their lines were non-bungee, ladder lines with a series of grab handles along them. They also had chunky brass trigger clips at each end. My running belt was a bulky contraption that fitted around my waist and looking back, I now see why running with dogs then hurt my back!

If a friendly and accessible user guide such as this had been available then, I am certain we would have been happier, safer, and saved significantly financially by not making costly, poor purchases.

In the years since, I stopped running for a bit, concentrating on other canine sports, but in late 2018 I revisited canicross and realised things had changed hugely. One significant change was increased specialisation in canisports and the advent of specialist retailers such as K9 Trail Time, offering superb support, advice and guidance. I had the huge pleasure and privilege of getting to know Emily and work with her during the isolation of a pandemic lockdown, running webinars for canisports newbies and chatting about canine science and nutrition regularly. Indeed, that time saw a boom in interest in canicross as a way to exercise dog and person. As a result, quality, supportive and effective advice to ensure canine and human health and well-being was hugely important – Emily was then and remains my 'go-to guru' for any of my own, or my clients' canisports needs, queries and purchases.

This book represents the culmination of not just a passion and deep interest in canicross, but also extensive experience in training, competing in and supporting canisports. Emily is dedicated to helping handlers ('mushers') make excellent choices for themselves and their dogs, with bespoke harness fitting services and advice, as well as offering educational resources and training opportunities. In addition to running a specialist canisports retail business, a canicross coaching business and an 'active dog academy', Emily is also a qualified canine hydrotherapist, so has more than an average appreciation for the importance of training, conditioning, rehabilitation and recovery for active dogs.

I know this book will be a valuable addition to the bookshelf or reading list of any active dog enthusiast. For anyone needing an accessible and user-friendly guide when starting out, this book encapsulates the essentials and provides scope for knowledge acquisition towards competitive events, longer distances and canisports challenges.

In the words of Emily, 'active dogs are happy dogs'. This book will allow you to support your dog's happiness with a great guide to canicross.

Hike on!

Dr Jacqueline Boyd
Animal Scientist, Canine Consultant, Cocker Spaniel Afficionado, Canicrosser

Emily's philosophy that active dogs are happy dogs underpins everything she does, encouraging dog owners to join their dogs exercising.

Canicross is the fun sport of cross-country running with your dog attached to you. It requires specific equipment and training.

# INTRODUCTION
# What is Canicross?

Canicross, when viewed through the eyes of a bystander, may look like a sport that is only available for certain people and certain breeds of dogs. Running with dogs is something that can be seen as being limited in its accessibility, and there are many myths surrounding canicross that I hope to dispel throughout this book. The canicross community is one of the most inclusive and welcoming in the dog world, and I look forward to sharing how canicross can help you and your dog find fun and fitness together.

## The History of Canicross

Canicross is known as an 'extreme' sport originating from dog sledding, when the dog kennel owners sought another activity to keep their sled dog teams fit during warmer months.

The original dogs pulling in harness were the traditional sled dog breeds, the most recognisable being Huskies and Malamutes, but there are many more. These dogs were doing a job alongside us, transporting goods on sleds across difficult winter terrain when vehicle access was limited, or impossible, due to the conditions.

Once the need for these teams of dogs required for transportation became less important in the twentieth century, the activity of dog sledding became more recreational, although it is thought that there have always been races connected to the sport.

When the dogs were retiring, or as part of a summer conditioning routine, the 'mushers,' as they are known, would attach the dogs to themselves to run. This meant more gentle exercise for the dogs and prevented them losing fitness, keeping their mental and physical stimulation going when they were unable to do their normal job.

The International Federation for Sleddog Sports (IFSS), the main global governing body for the sled dog sports including canicross, now classifies any breed of dog fit to run in a harness as a 'sled dog.'

It's not known exactly when canicross started to be developed as a sport, but it has been growing exponentially across Europe and the USA for over 20 years, with the most growth seen since the lockdowns of the COVID-19 pandemic.

During this time dog ownership figures rocketed, due to so many people working from home and making the decision to add a dog to their family.

**SLED DOG**

A sled dog is a dog, irrespective of the breed or type, capable of being harnessed and of competing in one of the classes listed in the IFSS Regulations without a potential, risk, to be calculated beforehand, of harming the dog's well-being.

(Taken from the IFSS Race Rules 2022–2024.)

Even the smallest of dogs can be considered a 'sled dog' under the international classification for the sport, so don't rule it out just because you have a small dog.

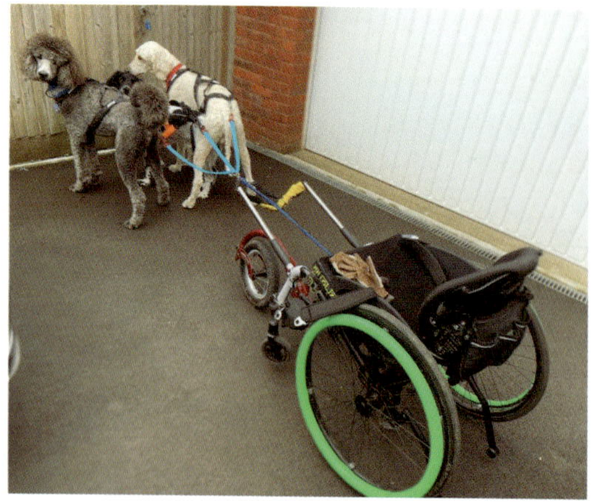

You don't need to be able to run to follow the principles of canicross training outlined in this book; you can do this at a slower speed and even from a wheelchair.

## What is Canicross?

Canicross in its most basic form involves running with your dog, but the key difference in 'running with your dog' and 'canicross' lies in the use of the specialised equipment, and the attachment of your dog to you.

The equipment includes a specifically designed harness to allow the dog full freedom of movement, a belt for the human, ergonomically fitted to distribute any pull force away from your back, and a bungee lead to absorb any pull between you. By attaching your dog to you via the harness, belt and bungee, you can form effective communication while promoting teamwork and strengthening the bond between you.

Canicross is generally thought to be trail running rather than road running, because the 'cross' element is cross country, where you and your dog can make the most of your running together, because it's far more mentally and visually stimulating to be out in the countryside.

If the running element of canicross is putting you off, everything in this book can be applied to canihiking too, which is canicross but walking instead of running, and might appeal to people who have more limited mobility or who don't feel that they are ready for running yet.

Throughout this book I will refer to canicross and running with your dog, but the benefits, equipment, principles of training and developing your bond with your dog, can all be found in walking with your dog using the canicross methods, and can also be applied for wheelchair users who want to give this incredible sport a go.

Specifically adapted cross-country wheelchairs can be used with your dog attached to you via a belt and bungee line, and even mobility chairs more suitable for urban terrain can be used; you would just need to consider the routes you choose for your dog.

## Why I Started Canicrossing

While I was not someone who wanted to run, let alone someone who wanted to run with my dog, circumstances led me to canicross when I adopted a highly active Husky Collie cross.

Tegan was not only reactive to dogs, but she also suffered with separation anxiety and I spent months trying different sports, and being asked to leave, before a friend suggested canicross. It didn't take long to see the benefits of running together and realise this was going to be our thing.

Tegan was more tired after our runs because she was having to focus on listening for my directions, using her brain as well as her body. We started to build up our fitness together, and I began to see a happier and more settled dog because we had found a way to connect through activity.

If I had done my research initially, then I should have realised that running would be the perfect activity to bond with my Husky (bred for endurance running in harness) crossed with Collie (bred for running all day working sheep), but it took me a while to figure that out. It took even longer to work out how to get the best experience from our running, and that's why I have written this book: to share with you all the things I wish I'd known from the beginning, to support you in your canicross journey with your dog, so you can enjoy running with your dog right from the start.

You can enjoy canicross and running achievements with your dog if you take the time to learn a little bit more about the sport before you get started.

## Your Why

Your reasons for reading this book on canicross will be personal to you. Everyone who canicrosses with their dog has their own story, their own history with their dog, and their own reasons for wanting to take part in this fun activity.

You might have a dog (like I did) who is driving you crazy with some unwanted behaviour, and you might be at your wits' end with it all, looking for the perfect solution. You might want to get fitter and healthier, and this might be a way to motivate yourself to get out there and discover a new sport with your dog that can help you both build stronger and fitter bodies for a longer future together.

You might want to connect with your dog more and develop your bond in a different way that interests you both. You might just want to save time and get yourself and your dog exercised in the minimum amount of time in the day, because we all lead busy lives.

Whatever your reason for wanting to get started, it will be very specific and very personal, and I hope to give you even more reasons to continue down this path.

Most people who start canicross will tell you they were struggling with some aspect of their dog's behaviour or exercise regime, and this led them to seek out an activity where they could still have fun with their dog, but keep them on the lead and safe.

People have many individual reasons for getting into canicross with their dogs, and everyone will start at different points in their life.

Looking at canicross from the outside, it is easy to see why people with more challenging dogs find the sport, because of the element of control you still retain over your dog when they are attached to you. Having a dog attached to you means they can't run off and chase the local wildlife, or worse, livestock. It also means you don't have the worry of them running into a road, or up to other people and their dogs. During the pandemic, when the price of dogs in the UK went up by over 50 per cent and similar increases were reported across the US, it also provided security that your dog wasn't about to be snatched away from you, at least not without a fight.

There are many obvious benefits of canicross for your dog, but some are more subtle. The list that follows is not exhaustive, but is generally recognised as containing the main reasons people choose canicross as a sport for themselves and their dogs.

## Benefits for Your Dog

### Physical Exercise

Canicross provides a great form of physical exercise for dogs. It allows them to release their pent-up energy, which can be particularly beneficial for high-energy breeds. Dogs were all bred with a purpose in mind and, while they may not be fulfilling their traditional breed purpose in your household, they will still need something to satisfy their need to run.

We know that dogs, being quadrupeds, are highly efficient at running – much more so than us – and as a result do not tire so easily from general running as we might. That explains why so many people have discovered that taking your dog for a bit of a run around the park is often not enough to then allow for a relaxing day at home. Many active dog owners report that their dogs will go home from a walk and immediately initiate play in the garden, as if they have not been exercised at all. There can be many reasons for this, but generally you will not be able to meet all your dog's exercise needs through a simple walk or run, which is where the mental stimulation that canicross provides will take effect.

### Mental Stimulation

Running connected to a person will engage your dog's mind more as they navigate the environment with you. Using voice cues ensures you are training at the same time as running, and switches on your dog's brain to concentrate on the cues.

You will be indicating to your dog what pace you're going to go at, which direction you're going to go in, and give them a focus for their running that you don't get if they are off lead and doing their own thing. The engagement of your dog's brain, to get them thinking and concentrating, satisfies another need for them and can help prevent destructive behaviours displayed in dogs who are bored.

## Socialisation

A huge benefit of canicross is that it allows dogs to interact with new dogs and people without being forced to engage with them. You might encounter numerous 'others' during your run, but you have the control to either prevent your dog from going

If you have found that regular walks are not meeting your dog's needs, then running with your dog could be the activity for you.

Safe interaction with other dogs is one of the reasons that canicross is looked upon as being a good sport for reactive dogs.

over to them, or stop others interfering with your dog. This type of interaction, from a distance, promoting healthy socialisation, can be incredibly useful in reducing fear or aggression towards unfamiliar individuals, and is one of the reasons that canicross is looked upon as a sport particularly suitable for nervous and reactive dogs.

## Reduced Stress and Improved Behaviour

The physical activity of running alone can help alleviate anxiety and stress in dogs. Research has shown that regular exercise for dogs who have general anxiety, can reduce anxiety-related behaviours; so, even if your dog is too nervous to contemplate running in a group or where others are, you can help your dog simply in the activity of canicross. A reduction in anxiety is also linked with an improvement in behaviour.

Tired dogs or 'fulfilled' dogs, are generally better behaved. Canicross can help reduce destructive behaviours such as chewing or digging, because your dog will lack the energy or motivation to partake in something that it's not been directed to do. Your dog will have had their mental and physical needs met and so they will not be looking for extracurricular activities. It also makes unwanted behaviours less appealing to your dog, because they have something much more exciting to focus on.

## Enhanced Obedience

As canicross is a sport that you need to train for, you will find that during the process of this training, your dog will learn to follow cues during canicross runs such as 'right', 'left' or 'steady'. These cues will be easily transferable into other activities of daily life, which can then translate into better obedience in different situations, so it's a win-win situation.

## Weight Management and Health

An additional benefit of regular canicross sessions is that physical exercise can help dogs maintain a healthy weight, or even lose any excess pounds, which is crucial for their overall health. The number of dogs considered to be obese in the UK by vets in 2022 was thought to be one in 14, but the

Dogs who are fulfilled both mentally and physically will be less likely to display unwanted behaviours, as they have a focus for their energy.

vets who were involved in reporting for the study, estimate this figure could be far higher. In the US, this figure is currently estimated at nearly 60 per cent. This is far from ideal and when you consider that obesity is the cause of so many conditions in both ourselves and our dogs, it is a benefit that cannot be overlooked. Closely connected to this is cardiovascular health.

Like humans, dogs benefit from cardiovascular exercise. Canicross can improve their heart and lung health, and I have personal experience of how having a fit and healthy dog through canicross can benefit them if they do end up with a condition. Both of my original Collie crosses developed mitral valve disease, and the consultant cardiologist said the fact they were so fit would only support the condition and prolong the declining effects of it.

It might seem obvious but it's worth noting as a benefit of canicross that running helps develop a dog's muscle strength and tone. Due to the nature of canicross being a sport in which dogs propel themselves forwards, the increase in muscle tone can often be seen in the hindquarters, which can aid mobility and reduce the risk of injury. Some dogs will develop very strong forequarters, as they use their shoulders to pull themselves forward in harness. Whichever style of running your dog has, the main benefit comes from the straight and stable technique of running that a dog will have when running in harness, and it's this which makes the benefits to the muscles of your dog unique to canicross.

## Enhanced Agility and Other Benefits

In cross-country running, you will inevitably be moving through varied terrain with natural obstacles, which can improve a dog's agility and coordination. We know that this coordination, known as proprioception, is very important for a dog's overall health and well-being. It is one of the less-discussed benefits of canicross, but one which will certainly help your dog, particularly as they move into old age.

Running with your dog can help support a longer healthier life for your dog, as the controlled exercise has many health benefits.

Typically, when canicrossing, you will start to expand your horizons with new routes that take you slightly further afield from your usual dog walking haunts. This will enable your dog to have the opportunity to explore new scents and environments, stimulating their senses, which is beneficial for their mental health.

It is well known that regular exercise is associated with a longer, healthier life for humans, and the same can be assumed for dogs. Canicross can contribute to this overall well-being and longevity by providing regular, controlled exercise, which facilitates good health.

Canicross involves strengthening muscles in your dog whilst in harness, which can help target areas of weakness.

Canicross is a shared activity that promotes trust, teamwork and builds a bond with the owner. Your dog will begin to look to you for everything fun and fulfilling, thereby strengthening your relationship and the trust they have in you.

Many dogs simply love running alongside their owners, and the enjoyment they get from this is a benefit in itself.

### Increased Awareness of Health

One of the things you will find as a result of starting to canicross is that you will begin to be more observant of your dog's behaviour, and you may start to notice things you hadn't previously. For example, because you end up behind your dog when they are running, you will notice subtle differences in the way they move, you will spot where they place their paws when they are in particular gaits, and you will start to build a bigger picture of your dog's overall health and well-being.

This attention to detail will allow you to pick up on differences in your dog before they become a problem, and you will potentially save yourself a lot of time at the vets by being able to accurately observe and record anything related to your dog's health.

## Benefits for You

We've extensively covered the benefits of canicross for your dog, but there are also many benefits for you. Your main goal might be to keep your dog fit, healthy and happy, but you can't ignore the fact that you are going to be a 50/50 partner in this sport.

The one thing I was unsure of when I first started running with my dogs was whether I would want to continue to do the sport once I'd got a bit fitter, as motivation for going to the gym or any other form of physical activity had always been very hit-and-miss for me.

Over the years, I have found that although there have been peaks and troughs in my motivation, the way I feel both physically and mentally

In sharing an activity with your dog in which you are both so involved, you will inevitably strengthen the bond between you.

when I'm regularly canicross training, means I don't think I will ever give it up now.

You may find that the first few weeks of training are tough, as you and your dog establish your own boundaries and capabilities within the sport, but almost everyone who tries canicross ends up falling headlong into it for the reasons I will outline below.

## Exercise Motivation and Improved Fitness

This is probably one of the most important benefits if you are someone like me who was never particularly motivated to take part in sport at school, college or in adult life. Canicross provides a strong incentive for people to get outside and exercise regularly, since they have a dedicated running partner who is always eager to go. The daily exercise needs of your dog provide a compelling reason for you to maintain a consistent workout routine. Your dog can be a mini-motivator, spurring you on with their endless energy and eagerness. Many people will say they can find numerous reasons not to do something, but if their dog is staring up at them with those 'puppy dog' eyes, they will find the energy and motivation to get out and go for a run.

Regular canicross running can help individuals improve their cardiovascular fitness, endurance and overall physical health. You need to develop core strength to be able to run with your dog, and improved balance and flexibility are benefits associated with cross-country running attached to your dog.

The obesity crisis is as critical in humans as it is in dogs. An NHS paper published in January 2023 indicated that almost three quarters of people aged 45–74 in England alone are overweight or obese. The World Obesity Atlas in 2023 predicted that as many as half of the global population will be overweight within twelve years if nothing is done. Canicross can be an effective way for people to manage or lose weight, as it

Whatever your starting point of fitness, you will also benefit from the additional motivation of running with your dog.

If you are looking for a fun way to lose weight, then canicross can help keep you going, particularly if you join in with group runs.

combines aerobic exercise with the added resistance of a pulling dog. This combination helps us to control weight while taking part in something fun and stimulating with our dogs, so can benefit those who have otherwise struggled with their weight and fitness.

## Mental Well-Being and Other Benefits

It might seem obvious, but the impact that running with a dog can have on mental health should not be underestimated. Running is known for reducing stress and anxiety while promoting relaxation and happiness through the release of endorphins. With the rise in mental health issues and reports of one in six people suffering with some form of anxiety or depression in the UK, it is safe to assume this is a growing problem. It is widely suggested that pets have a positive impact on mental health, but when you factor in canicross too, you have a winning combination for nurturing a better outlook on life.

When they start canicross, most people try to find a group to begin with, as local groups can offer support and encouragement. The canicross groups or events provide opportunities to meet like-minded people and make new friends, which can be a bonus for someone who is more isolated by the recent trend of working from home or in a smaller team.

One of the reasons I decided to take up canicross was that running with your dog allows you to combine your own exercise routine with your dog's, making it a time-efficient way to stay active. During pandemic lockdowns, when in the UK we were only allowed out once during the day, canicross was the perfect solution to get yourself and your dog exercised at the same time and, as a bonus, it also met the government guidelines.

When you are running with a dog, you get encouraged to explore new trails, parks and natural areas, adding variety to your exercise routine. If you meet with a group, someone usually leads the run, and so you can benefit from other people's knowledge of previously unexplored routes.

## Safety, Enjoyment and Improving Communication

Runners, and in particular women runners, can often feel intimidated by trail running solo. Canicross can provide an added layer of safety during outdoor runs, as your dog offers protection and companionship.

Canicross is a fun and enjoyable way to exercise, particularly if you are not self-motivated to go out and run, as you can share the experience with your dog. Many people do not enjoy running without dogs and while they may, on occasion, run solo, they much prefer the enhanced experience

Exploring new trails in your locality with other people can be a great way to see parts of the countryside you never even knew existed.

of running with their dogs. To take the emphasis away from your own running form and technique as you concentrate on your dog is an effective way to distract yourself from any negative thoughts about it.

If you are spending more time with your dog, particularly when you are exercising and training together regularly, you will begin to develop your communication skills with them. Canicross involves training voice cues to ensure you don't encounter any problems when running attached to your dog, and within this training you will learn what motivates your dog and what they respond to, which you can transfer into any other training you do.

When you begin to observe your dog canicrossing you will also learn more about them, their personality, when they are feeling their best, and recognise their limits too. This knowledge can help you to determine their overall picture of health and has undoubtably changed the relationship that many people have with their dog, because they find it easier to spot the little behavioural changes when they are working so closely in partnership.

## SUMMARY

- Canicross is a relatively new sport, which is growing rapidly and requires specific training and equipment to take part safely.
- The popularity of canicross is largely due to its accessibility for people and dogs of all different ages, sizes and fitness levels.
- Everyone has a different and individual reason for wanting to take part in canicross.
- The many benefits of canicross for dogs are very similar to the benefits for people.
- Running with your dog can improve physical and mental health for both of you, and lead to a better relationship with your dog.

Before you get started canicrossing, there are some questions you might have to determine to ensure that the sport is suitable for you and your dog.

# CHAPTER 1
# Canicross Basics

Now you have established all the different reasons for taking part in canicross, you might be wondering if you can canicross with your own dog. Many people have doubts about their own level of fitness or that of their dog before they start canicrossing, and this is where I've seen the biggest myths surrounding canicross, which puts people off even beginning the sport. This chapter dispels those myths and discusses the inclusivity of running with your dog.

Your canicross dog is not necessarily going to have been bred for the pulling sports, so you need to be mindful they may have genetic predispositions that require a longer period of time for them to fully develop for the sport.

## Canicross: A Sport for Everyone?

First, the consensus is that any person, of any age, can start canicross and the same can be said of the dog, with a few notable exceptions.

Puppies should not be canicrossing. Until a dog is thought to be fully grown, they should not be pulling in a harness. There is a rule which circulates that there should be 5 minutes of exercise per month of age for puppies. That 'rule' has been challenged as unrealistic, particularly for dogs of breeds who have working backgrounds. You would not expect a working Border Collie to be doing only an hour's worth of work at a year old. You would also not expect them to be exercised for a short period of time, then suddenly, when they come of age, be thrown into a full day's work with no gradual build-up or conditioning of the dog for the job.

The same can be said for canicross. There are many things you can do pre-adulthood to train your dog for canicross, including teaching all your voice cues and general socialisation. You can also be doing activities which lend themselves to canicross training, so things like on-lead walking in a harness where you allow your dog to pull are important to incorporate into your weekly regime of exercise.

The sled dog world, specifically people who are training their dogs within teams for longer distances, will often start to train their dogs in harness from six months old onwards. It needs to be noted here that these dogs have been bred for the endurance activities they are taking part in; they are always going to be part of a team and so the pressure on these dogs is shared with more experienced members of the team, who can guide them and take the majority share of the work while the younger dogs are learning.

Whilst it's acceptable to get your puppy used to a harness, they should not be pulling in one until they are fully grown in their bodies and minds.

The dogs who are canicrossing with you are likely to be individual dogs. Perhaps you might want to run with two, but generally, it will be one dog and so the pressure to pull, learn the voice cues and respond accordingly will fall solely on them. This does need to be considered, because the situation is very different and often 'pet' canicross dogs are not dogs who have been bred for the sport and therefore may not be genetically set up for starting the sport at a young age.

## Dogs: Who Can Take Part?

### Breed of Dog

One common misconception is that only certain sizes or breeds of dogs can participate in canicross. However, canicross is open to all sizes of dogs, including small breeds such as Cocker Spaniels, Jack Russell Terriers and even Dachshunds. The physical capability of the dog is the primary consideration, and any breed can take part as long as they are in good health and not at risk of harm.

Large breeds should not be excluded either. Breeds like Wolfhounds, Malamutes and Great Danes have been seen participating in canicross successfully. The key is to ensure that the dog's well-being is not compromised by the activity.

Overall, you will know if your dog is capable of running, able to breathe efficiently and cool itself down effectively. Some brachycephalic breeds, such as Pugs, can get quite hot and overheat due to their limited nasal cavity for evaporative cooling through panting. Therefore, it's important to be aware of potential restrictions based on breed and conformational issues.

For example, French Bulldogs have been bred in a way that compromises their movement. This is a sad consequence of selective breeding, as they are genetically capable of running, but not efficiently. While most dogs can run without interruption for much longer than humans, certain conformational issues can make it more challenging for some dogs, causing them to tire more quickly. This may make them less suitable for canicross. If you have concerns, it is advisable to have a conversation with your vet, who can provide valuable insights based on your dog's individual circumstances.

Your canicross dog can be any breed that is fit and healthy; the size of the dog is not as important in canicross as their physical ability to run.

### Age

Age is an important factor to consider when determining who can take part in canicross. Once a dog is fully grown, you can start introducing them to pulling in a harness. However, the age at which a dog is considered fully grown varies depending on size and breed, leading to debates about the appropriate age to start running with dogs.

Some people suggest waiting until the dog is 18 months old before engaging in any activities, while others believe training in harness can commence as early as six months. A middle ground approach can be taken, where voice cue training begins as soon as the dog is taken out for walks, following their vaccination schedule. Voice cues such as 'left', 'right', and 'straight on' can be taught to establish a foundation for future canicross training. It is important to ensure that the dog's growth plates have closed before engaging in any strenuous activities.

Older dogs can also enjoy canicross, provided they are not pushed beyond their comfort and capability. It is not uncommon for dogs considered past their prime to participate in the sport.

Older dogs can safely take part in canicross provided you closely monitor their health and ensure they are exercising within their comfort and capability.

However, it is crucial to monitor their well-being and ensure they genuinely enjoy the activity without being subjected to unnecessary strain. Consultation with your vet can help determine the suitability of older dogs for canicross.

Puppies, on the other hand, should not be involved in running in harness as they are still growing, and the physical demands can be too much for their developing bodies. Generally, dogs under the age of twelve months are not allowed to participate in races. The International Federation for Sleddog Sports (IFSS) and other race organisations follow an age restriction of eighteen months. This decision aligns with the belief that proper training should precede participation in races, ensuring the dog's well-being and readiness. Starting with gradual and incremental distances is recommended, considering the impact of the harness and load on the dog's biomechanics.

A dog's growth plates are regions of bone in a growing dog which result in the lengthening of the bone and therefore the limb. The growth plates close at a similar age in the same size of dog, so around eight months in very small breeds and up to eighteen months in giant breeds. Common sense would suggest that any rigorous physical activity should be kept to a minimum until these growth plates have fully developed and closed for your dog.

Although there have been many debates on the exact age you should start to run a dog in harness, there have been no studies to support any particular age, which leads to the conclusion that every dog should be treated as an individual and every factor of that dog's health and well-being taken into account before your dog is asked to run with you in harness.

It is essential to carefully consider both the age at which you start your dog in canicross and the age at which you retire them. While dogs of various ages can partake in canicross, pushing older dogs beyond their limits may compromise their comfort and safety. It is crucial to observe and assess your dog's enjoyment and physical condition. Seeking advice from your vet regarding the appropriate age to start or retire your dog from canicross can provide valuable guidance based on their individual needs and circumstances.

## Case Study: Atlanta Tideswell and Raven's Story

Raven (a German Shepherd dog) and I started to canicross together last year and we love it. I got Raven when she was eight weeks old and she has been terrified of everything since I got her home. Raven is a fear reactive dog and has to be muzzled around people and dogs. She unfortunately bit one of my family members out of fear. I've had lots of trainers who haven't been able to help. I messaged the breeder and all she had to say was that I should put her to sleep (which obviously wasn't going to happen). She became so difficult to control that I even put her up for rehoming. Thankfully, with canicross she focuses more on the job she's doing and this has built her confidence up massively, as well as my own. I know that when she reacts, I tense up. By doing canicross I feel I can relax and enjoy my time with her, without looking over my shoulder for people or dogs. It's made our bond so much stronger. She doesn't react when she's in her harness and focused on moving forwards. She gets so excited whenever I pick up our bag to go, as she now knows it's one thing where she can be free and enjoy time out and about. I couldn't have dreamt it would be like this over a year ago. She has grown massively into the almost-confident dog I know she can be.

As stated above, Raven is a very fear reactive dog, in that she would bite if someone came too close and invaded her space. With canicross she has calmed down massively and is now focused on the job in hand. She even passes dogs and people with no reaction. I was also lacking in a lot of confidence, especially with being able to control Raven; however, my cani coach assured me everything will be okay, and she will do everything to help. Raven now even loves her and doesn't like her leaving.

Atlanta and her German Shepherd, Raven, who have found a way to bond and overcome Raven's reactivity around both people and dogs through canicross.

## Limitations for Your Dog

### Anxious Dogs

Dogs who have issues with anxiety might struggle to cope with the demands of the sport of canicross. If your dog is anxious around other dogs and people, or has specific anxieties related to things you might come across in a canicross environment, then you may want to consider if canicross will be right for your dog.

### Reactive Dogs

This is the one I personally hear more about than any other concern when it comes to running with dogs, as people are unsure about canicross with dogs who are reactive. Canicross is widely recognised as a sport that is suitable for dogs who are reactive, and I have even listed it as a benefit because it can help to reduce a dog's reactivity in certain situations. However, this doesn't necessarily mean that canicross will be suitable for all reactive dogs, and we will look at this in more depth.

### Limiting Physical Conditions

Our dogs, like us, can have physical disabilities that may prevent them doing certain activities. For example, if you have a dog who is blind, they might not be able to take part in agility because they will not have the awareness of the course to be able to negotiate the obstacles safely.

Canicross is different in this respect because the dogs are all under close control and attached to us, so we are much better able, with a few training tweaks, to manage the situation to allow a blind dog to take part.

Another physical disability which people ask about is if they can they take part with their deaf dog. The short answer is yes and with adaption to the training cues, many deaf dogs can take part in and enjoy canicrossing with their owners. While the below list is not exhaustive, there are many dogs who have the following conditions and are able to canicross with careful management:

- obesity
- arthritis
- hip or elbow dysplasia
- spondylosis
- epilepsy
- mitral valve disease (heart condition).

These dogs have all been found canicrossing under the watchful eye of a vet, and with an owner who recognises they need to monitor and regularly re-assess their dog's health with professionals for them to continue to enjoy the sport.

### More than One Dog

Another question frequently asked is if you can run with more than one dog. You can run with as many dogs as you like, but I'd strongly suggest not starting out with more than one. If you're going to make mistakes, then it's better to do it with one dog at a time; you are at a higher risk of injury with more weight attached to you.

Running with two dogs can be a lot of fun, but it is always better to start your training with one dog at a time, so if you make any mistakes, you can correct them more easily.

If you have an experienced canicross dog, you can help a more nervous or inexperienced dog learn the ropes by running them together.

## Humans: Who Can Take Part?

One of the more common barriers I hear to starting the sport of canicross is that people with a higher BMI (Body Mass Index) than that which is considered healthy feel that it's only people who are already slim, fit and healthy who can join in. I am one of those people and I had to be convinced that I wasn't going to be laughed out of any canicross group, because the thought of me being involved in a 'running' club was hilarious to me. I was encouraged, however, and although I started out on my own, the difference that it made to my health and fitness was enough to encourage me to join others after a period of time.

I lost three stone within three months of starting to run with my dog Tegan, and while my weight has always fluctuated, because I enjoy pretending that running means you can eat whatever you like, I have never gone back to my pre-canicross weight or size.

It is a common theme amongst canicrossers that weight loss and consistent weight loss is part of taking up a sport which encourages you to participate regularly.

### Case Study: Erin Fidler

I started canicross in Feb 2022 to lose weight. Over the years I've always tried to lose weight and then put it back on a few months later. By chance, I saw a canicross group running in my area and went along to a beginners run, and I was hooked! Honey suddenly became my ultimate PT. She immediately pulled and barked her head off, loving it, and that just gave me the inspiration to keep going. Knowing you're not going running alone, and that you are making your dog happy just made it so much easier. We started Couch to 5k in February and by the end of the year I had lost 3 stones, and we ran our first half marathon (in the snow!) in December. Along the way, we have made best friends and created a whole new lifestyle for ourselves, now spending all our spare time running long distances, hiking mountains or travelling round the UK with our canicross friends.

Erin and her dog Honey, who have both found a whole new lifestyle as a result of canicross and the motivation that running together brings.

If one of the things that has held you back so far is that you feel because you are above the recommended healthy BMI you cannot take part, then please do reconsider this. Many of the people involved have experienced this self-doubt, and once they started canicrossing or canihiking, have realised this isn't a barrier to enjoying the sport even from the start – and have often lost weight because of the increased activity.

## People Who Are Unfit

In a similar way, if you haven't been exercising for several years and feel that are you are too unfit to take part in a new sport which is mainly defined by running, this need not be a barrier. Canicross has a variety of paths into it, and the two most clearly defined groups of people who start the sport are either runners who want to enjoy their hobby with their dog or (and I think this is more common, particularly at the grass roots level), dog owners who are looking for a way to improve their health and bond with their dog.

If you go along to any of the canicross group runs or social events, most of the participants are not your average 'gym bunny', but more commonly people who have no other significant sporting or exercise interests, and have chosen canicross because it allows them to spend time

You don't have to look like a runner to start canicrossing with your dog; part of the fun of canicross can be the journey you take to get fitter and healthier together.

with their dog and other like-minded people in a relaxed and fun environment. So don't let any preconceptions about the level of fitness you need to have before you start put you off giving it a go.

## Age

Similar to dogs, people of any age can partake in canicross as long as they are fully developed. It is worth noting that attaching a dog to your body during canicross adds an additional impact that must be considered. Even if you are a fit and healthy runner, running with a dog introduces new challenges and impacts the body differently. This is especially true if your dog pulls or if you have a heavier dog that affects your balance while running.

Contrary to common misconceptions, older runners often excel in canicross due to their core stability and life experiences. Strength is often more crucial than fitness when starting out, so individuals already participating in other activities incorporating strength-building exercises can begin their canicross journey without hesitation.

Children should be introduced to canicross very carefully due to the additional strain it places on their developing bodies. Parents should consider both the child's size and the size of the dog when deciding if they are a suitable match. It is crucial not to overburden young children or teenagers with dogs that are too strong or energetic for them to handle. Dogs should always be matched appropriately with the person, regardless of age or physical development, to prevent injuries.

## People with Medical Conditions

While there are many people with medical considerations who take part in canicross, you should avoid canicross if your medical condition is aggravated by exercise or physical activity. It is vital to be mindful of any existing limitations that may prevent you from safely participating in canicross. As mentioned earlier, the additional strain on the body during canicross requires a gradual approach and building up strength and fitness over time. Taking things slowly and working within the parameters of your condition, as well as your dog's condition, will allow for an enjoyable and injury-free canicross experience.

People of all ages can enjoy canicross, and even medical conditions need not always be a barrier to exercising with your dog.

## The Canicross Season

When I tell people that there is a canicross season, many people automatically assume that this is through the spring and summer months into autumn, when the weather is generally considered better and we have more light in our days. However, almost the opposite is true, and our 'season' tends to run from September to April or May, right through the winter months. The reason for this is again based on the sled dog heritage that the sport of canicross comes from.

Traditionally, all the sled dog races would have been winter sports and because (initially at least) canicross was a class added into a sled dog event, the races would have all been through the winter too. This is forgetting that canicross was used to keep dogs in condition through the warmer months and doesn't consider the fact that running as a sport is embraced by more people during the lighter and warmer months.

### Can You Canicross all Year Round?

The answer is not straightforward and must be based on the individual dog and the conditions on any given day you want to go and run with your dog. We all know the 'dogs die in hot cars' campaigns and how dangerous it can be for dogs to be shut in a small space in the heat; but how many of us think our dogs can die just from being outside on a warmer day and partaking in a bit of exercise?

## Temperature Comparison Chart

| | Celcius | Fahrenheit | Humidity |
|---|---|---|---|
| Fahrenheit + Humidity = Less than 110 - this equals max temp + humidity | 15 | 59 | 51 |
| Fahrenheit + Humidity = Less than 110 - this equals max temp + humidity | 14 | 57 | 53 |
| Fahrenheit + Humidity = Less than 110 - this equals max temp + humidity | 13 | 55 | 55 |
| Fahrenheit + Humidity = Less than 110 - this equals max temp + humidity | 12 | 53 | 57 |
| Fahrenheit + Humidity = Less than 110 - this equals max temp + humidity | 11 | 52 | 58 |
| Fahrenheit + Humidity = Less than 110 - this equals max temp + humidity | 10 | 50 | 60 |
| Fahrenheit + Humidity = Less than 110 - this equals max temp + humidity | 9 | 48 | 62 |
| Fahrenheit + Humidity = Less than 110 - this equals max temp + humidity | 8 | 46 | 64 |
| Fahrenheit + Humidity = Less than 110 - this equals max temp + humidity | 7 | 44 | 66 |
| Fahrenheit + Humidity = Less than 110 - this equals max temp + humidity | 6 | 43 | 67 |
| Fahrenheit + Humidity = Less than 110 - this equals max temp + humidity | 5 | 41 | 69 |
| Fahrenheit + Humidity = Less than 110 - this equals max temp + humidity | 4 | 39 | 71 |
| Fahrenheit + Humidity = Less than 110 - this equals max temp + humidity | 3 | 37 | 73 |
| Fahrenheit + Humidity = Less than 110 - this equals max temp + humidity | 2 | 35 | 75 |

This is an example of a temperature comparison chart, which gives maximum 'safe' figures for running sled dogs. This, however, might not be relevant for your dog as an individual and I recommend observing your own dog for safety.

The research has shown that dogs can suffer from what is known as 'heat-related illness' at any time of the year, but is recorded most often in the summer months, which seems logical.

Dogs who are unfit, overweight, dark-coated dogs, male dogs and dogs of certain breeds are more likely to suffer from a heat-related illness than others. You must look at your dog as an individual and assess the weather conditions on the day before deciding if it is ok to run with your dog.

There is a chart which gives a multiplication of temperature x humidity and if the factors combined exceed 110, then it is deemed unsafe for that dog to run in; however, some dogs will not be able to cope with this 'safe' temperature combination, while others may be able to run in conditions which far exceed the arbitrary 110 figure given. Humidity is the biggest problem for dogs, as high humidity prevents a dog being able to cool itself effectively; so even at some of the lower temperatures, if the humidity is high, this can cause your dog to overheat more quickly.

The best thing to do if you are not sure if you should be running your dog because it is warm, is to not take the risk. Once you begin to exercise more with your dog, you will start to notice their tolerance levels for temperatures, and with this knowledge you can then start to make judgements for your dog as an individual.

### Indications of a Problem

Things to look out for that may indicate that your dog is beginning to struggle in the higher temperatures or humidity are restlessness, seeking out cool areas or shade, looking to lie down, excessive panting, excess salivation and thick sticky saliva. Also look for glazed eyes, red or very pale pink (rather than healthy pink) gums, stiffness in movement which can lead to staggering, and any anxiety or agitation. There is also an increase in core body temperature and an increase in heart rate, although if you were exercising your dog, you may not be able to monitor this.

You should also avoid canicrossing in very cold weather conditions, or in windy, rainy conditions if you have a thin-coated dog who may struggle to keep warm, particularly if you are both starting out and need to stop regularly. If you see your dog shivering excessively, or experiencing any stiffness, lethargy, confusion and pale gums, then you should abort your run and get them back to a warm environment as soon as possible, gradually warming them back up.

Exercising your dog in warmer temperatures needs careful consideration and route planning to include safe water stops.

## Canicrossing in the Dark

Canicross does not necessarily need to be a daytime-only sport; there are many reasons why you might end up canicrossing in the dark, before or after work in the winter when the daylight hours are limited, or in the summer when it is cooler before or after the sun is out. You can choose when to fit your canicrossing into your routine, and if you do decide you will be going out in the dark, there are many ways you can still make it safe and fun.

You can get head torches for yourself, lights for your dog, and reflective running gear for both dog and human, all of which will make you more visible and increase your safety when canicrossing in the dark.

Canicrossing in the dark can be great fun, make yourself and your dog as visible as possible, so you can see and be seen.

### SUMMARY

- Canicross is open and accessible to most people and most dogs.
- You don't need to have a particular breed or size of dog to take part.
- You don't need to be fit before you start canicrossing.
- Care should be taken to ensure you and your dog won't be harmed by taking up the sport of canicross.
- You can canicross or canihike throughout the year if done carefully.
- Canicross can fit into your life around your work and other commitments.

Canicross equipment needs to be comfortable and fit for purpose, designed to support you both in your adventures.

# CHAPTER 2
# Canicross Equipment

The essential equipment required for canicross can be found in three main elements. The harness for your dog, the belt for yourself and the bungee line to connect you both. Selecting the right harness, belt, and bungee line suitable for you both, ensures your safety and comfort but it can be tricky to choose if you are new to the sport. If you source the correct kit, you can expect it to last for a number of years, so it is worthwhile taking the time to research the options before investing.

This chapter will guide you on how to choose the best equipment and fit for you both, so you don't make any costly mistakes when choosing it.

The basic canicross kit you will need is a properly fitted harness for your dog, a comfortable belt to distribute pull for yourself and a bungee line to connect you.

With the rise in popularity of canicross, there are now many different brands and styles of equipment that might be suitable for you and your dog.

## The Harness

When it comes to canicross, choosing the right harness is crucial. Dog sport harnesses are specifically designed to provide strength and functionality without causing discomfort or hindering the dog's movement. The key is to find the one that suits your dog's anatomy and causes the least amount of restriction.

The only style of harness which can potentially damage dogs, reportedly (but not scientifically proven) causing bicep injuries, are the harnesses which have straps that come across the front of the dog's shoulder and prevent forward movement of the shoulder. The harness is so important because a dog is structurally set up to be front loaded; a normal dog's weight distribution is 60 per cent in the forelimbs and 40 per cent in the hind limbs, so it is paramount you ensure your dog's forelimbs are always free to move with a full range of motion.

Choosing a canicross harness is probably the thing that dog owners new to the sport get most confused by, as there are now so many options available in different styles, materials and colours.

### Cost

A dog harness for canicross will be something that you will need to choose based on the fit and function for your dog as an individual, but you can expect to pay anything from £25–£90 ($32–$115) for a good-quality dog sports harness. You may be able to find cheaper options on big online retail sites, but the age-old adage 'buy cheap, buy twice' certainly applies to canicross harnesses. You can often pick up second-hand equipment on specific selling groups on social media and sometimes groups, clubs and coaches will have kit they can lend you to get you started, to ensure this is something you want to do before you splash out.

### What You Need to Know

Sled dog harnesses were traditionally the X-back design, which you will see on Huskies pulling sleds, and while these are excellent harnesses for this job, there are a few things about an X-back which might mean they don't suit your dog.

X-back harnesses were designed for a dog pulling a sled with a low point of pull. The dog would also have been running as part of a team and would always have been trained to run straight out in front with minimal sharp turns. The movement of the dog is very much a flowing rhythm and these harnesses are perfect for that.

The next thing to note about the X-back is that it is designed for the anatomy of a Husky and, while you might think that a dog is a dog, when you consider all the different breeds now taking part in canicross, you can see why these harnesses might not work for some breeds.

It can be very hard to find an X-back harness to fit a dog such as a Beagle or a Spaniel, as both

X-back harnesses were designed to fit a traditional sled dog breed, but they work on many other dog breeds for pulling too.

these breeds tend to be anatomically shorter in the body than a Husky. It can also be difficult at times, fitting deep-chested breeds such as the Dobermann or the German Short-haired Pointer, because the depth of the dog's chest takes up the length of the harness and alters the fit, so it doesn't sit as it should on the dog's back.

If you are reading this and thinking that your dog is a weird shape, then you are not alone and most canicrossers struggle to find something that works perfectly for their dog without guidance.

### Alternative Styles

There are lots of different harness styles, but you can generally place all harnesses into three categories: short-, mid- and long-style.

All these styles will usually have a fixed neck, so it will need to go over your dog's head, unlike some of the walking styles which have clips all over to secure it around your dog. This can cause problems for dogs who don't like having something squeezed over their head or ears, but with sympathetic training and lots of rewards, most dogs will come to realise the harness signifies a good thing and will not be fazed by the harness going over their head.

What you need to remember is that with a fixed neck there are no pressure points where one part of the harness is bulkier than the rest. You are more likely to get a comfortable fit for your dog to pull into with this type of neck than something which has clips or sliders on straps that could potentially dig in.

### A Short-Style Harness

Many canicrossers now choose to run their dogs in a short-style harness, which has always been known as an H-back style, because the harness

Short-style harnesses can all be similar to look at, but there are plenty of small design differences which can make one harness more suitable for your dog than another.

looks more like a walking harness and has one piece that runs centrally down the dog's spine. The shorter styles of harness now take different forms and are recognised by brand rather than a general style, but they all have similar attributes and benefit certain types of dogs. Breeds that may suit a short harness range from Terriers through to Great Danes.

Even short-style harnesses, designed for dog sports, should be made with a longer piece under the chest of the dog, that a regular harness will not have, with the aim of sitting further behind the front legs of your dog and leaving their legs more space to swing backwards and forwards when running.

A regular walking harness, if not restricting across the shoulders, could be fine if you are just looking to try out canicross to give you an idea if your dog is going to pull or not. Generally, however, not only are the walking harnesses a bit too restrictive for canicross, but they are also heavier in material, not as strong in construction and therefore more liable to break than a specifically designed sports harness. It is also worthwhile having a specific harness for canicross if you also use a harness for walking or other activities, to indicate to your dog the different expectations you will have of them in each harness.

## The Benefits

A shorter harness will give you more control over your dog because the attachment point for your bungee line is further up, closer to your dog's shoulders. This might be of benefit to people who are running with a reactive or nervous dog, who need to keep their dog closer to them.

A short harness will also mean that your dog doesn't have a lot of excess material flapping around over its back. Some dogs will not like having material over their spine or near their tail, and

Shorter harnesses with two clips are great for dogs who don't like having to pick their paws up to have a harness fitted.

this can cause your dog to move very differently if they react to the feeling of the longer harness over their back.

Most short-style harnesses will have one or two clips around the chest, which can mean that if your dog doesn't like having their paws touched to pick them up, they don't have to for the harness to be fitted. In some cases, dogs will even crouch down and 'creep' along the floor to avoid the feel of the long style of harness, which might be funny to witness but isn't funny for your dog, and would certainly cause them problems if they moved this way for any period of time.

The aim of canicross is to train your dog to run out in front and pull, but if your dog isn't particularly motivated to do this, and some dogs aren't natural pulling breeds, then a short-style harness will mean they can take things at their pace without extra material, designed to be pulled into, bunching up and creating an untidy mess of excess webbing on your dog's back.

If your dog isn't pulling out in front of you in a longer style harness, the harness can bunch up and flap around on your dog's back.

## The Disadvantages

If you're thinking that you'll just get a short-style harness to avoid any of the problems associated with a long-style harness, then you need to be aware that there are some disadvantages to the shorter harness.

The shorter style will usually mean that the harness has clips to secure it to your dog and this can be a point of weakness in a harness. Every dog sports harness will have tried-and-tested clips but if you stand on them, trap them in a door, or otherwise compromise their integrity, unless you are checking your kit every time you use it, you may create a weakness that you don't notice until it breaks.

The shorter harnesses will also always cover the spine of your dog behind the shoulders. The design of them (think H-back) means this is the support for the harness and so if your dog has a particularly sensitive back or flexible spine, the feeling of the material might cause them to move differently in the harness.

The biggest issue that people encounter with short-style harnesses, however, is that the pull of the harness is always directed back from the top. What this means is that if the harness doesn't fit quite right, or your dog is a very strong puller, the harness has the potential to ride up into the soft fleshy part of your dog's throat and cause a wheezing noise. Essentially your dog's airways become compromised by the pressure of the harness.

This is most often a problem in strong pulling breeds who also tend to carry their head low when they are running; think of a Spaniel who runs with a very low head carriage because they scent while they are running. Also Border Collies are genetically predisposed to carry themselves low when they are running, so they can be affected by this too.

If your dog is a more athletic breed that pulls strongly, a shorter harness might ride up on your dogs' neck and restrict your dog's airway.

## A Long-Style Harness

The X-back is a great example of a longer style of running harness, designed to distribute the weight of the sled being towed down the length of the dog's body, and out at the attachment point for the bungee line, which is situated near the base of the dog's tail if properly fitted. The common theme with the longer style of harness is that they will all have this distribution of the force of your dog pulling near the base of the tail, and will need to be fitted for the whole length of your dog's body correctly.

### The Benefits

The long-style harness will always direct any pull on your dog down, away from the throat and put the force through your dog's chest, which is a much stronger structural area for them to feel the harness pull against, rather than the neck or shoulder groove.

The fact that the harness is distributing the force through longer straps means it is dissipated along the length of the dog and not positioned just behind the shoulders; so for dogs who pull hard, this would mean that there will be less tension in the shoulder area, and less risk of sore muscles from overload here. The long-style harness will also generally be made as one piece, so there are no points of weakness in it. This is particularly beneficial with strong dogs who might otherwise break clips or straps on regular harnesses.

### The Disadvantages

Any longer harness will usually be made of uninterrupted material, so there are no weak points in the harness, which can be a disadvantage if you have a dog who doesn't like to pick their feet up to have a harness fitted. There is a trick with some dogs if they're ok with the harness fitting snugly over their head, whereby you get them to step

A long-style harness will distribute a stronger pull better along the body of your dog.

into it on the floor and work the harness up and over their head. However, this is sometimes more stressful than just training them to pick their feet up for the harness.

The long-style harnesses can also be harder to get a correct fit on your dog, because there are no adjustment points and therefore the different elements of the harness must fit the different anatomical points on your dog's body correctly without any adjustment. With all the different breeds of dogs who canicross, this isn't always easy.

Mentioned as a benefit of the shorter harnesses, the excess material that is in the harness design is a disadvantage of the longer style because of the extra material which might flap about if your dog isn't pulling hard into the harness all the time. This can put a more anxious or insecure dog off pulling into it; if when they drop back it feels strange, the most extreme reaction is to stop altogether.

### A Mid-Length Harness

The mid-length harness tends to be a hybrid of the two different styles. The most important thing to note though, is that most harnesses categorised as mid-length work in the same way as the longer harnesses do, directing pull underneath and along the side of the dog's body, but don't extend over the dog's hips and have an attachment point before the base of the tail.

The harness will be more suitable for dogs who pull hard but for whatever reason don't fit into a longer harness, as there is less length to have to fit correctly on the dog's body. A mid-length harness may also be more suitable for a dog who has issues in the hip region and needs a harness that doesn't interfere in this area, but who still pulls strongly when running.

The disadvantages of a mid-length harness include the fact some of the harnesses should be pulled into, to maintain its design integrity and they can look strange when being fitted for dogs who are not always straight out in front.

A mid-length harness is perfect for a dog who might be a strong puller, but doesn't fit into or suit a long-style harness.

### Material

The material used for dog sports harnesses should be lightweight, durable and preferably waterproof or water-resistant. The harness may be padded, and a balance should be found between padding for comfort and less material for non-restriction and breathability.

Fleece was originally the most-used material but fleece can hold water, mud and end up causing rubbing on your dog's skin. With the development of newer, more suitable materials, the harnesses are now made from various ripstop materials much better suited to the mud and wet weather that most of us end up canicrossing in.

Harnesses, belts and lines can usually all be washed carefully on low temperatures in your washing machine if put inside a washing bag or pillow case, to prevent damage to clips. This helps to keep your kit in good condition.

## Harness Fit

Once you have chosen a style of harness you think will suit your dog, the next thing you need to do is to make sure it fits. It has already been mentioned that some breeds will not fit particular styles of harness, and this is due to their anatomy. I have developed a simple five-star system for harness fitting that works for any breed of dog and any harness, so you can quickly identify if the harness you have selected is going to be a comfortable fit for your dog. There are a few bony landmarks that you can use on any dog to determine harness fit, and it is worth getting familiar with these so you can be your own harness fitter.

A well-fitted dog sports harness will work with your dog's shape to distribute any pulling force comfortably along your dog's body.

## The Main Bony Landmarks

### Shoulder Bone

The scapula is the big, flat bone that connects to the top of the humerus bone in your dog's front leg. The scapula is involved in the movement of the front leg. You can feel the scapula if you stroke down from the base of your dog's neck on their back, towards the top of the front leg.

### Point of Shoulder

This is where your dog's scapula meets the humerus and forms a little bony notch on the front of your dog's leg around where the neck meets the chest.

### Breastbone

The manubrium (the front of the sternum, or breastbone) is the point at which your dog's ribs end in the front of the chest. The manubrium can be felt if you run your hand down the front of your dog's neck and you will feel a small nobble of bone centrally located between the front legs.

### Chest

Your dog's ribs connect down from the spine to form the chest. In a healthy dog you should be able to feel the ribs under the skin but not see them too prominently. If you feel back along your dog's rib cage, you will come to what feels like a half rib at the very end, this is known as the floating rib and being able to identify where this is will help with harness fitting.

### Hip Bones

Your dog's sacrum is the big hip bone structure located above your dog's hind legs, and you should be able to feel the two points of the wings of the ilium above the hip socket in a dog of a healthy weight.

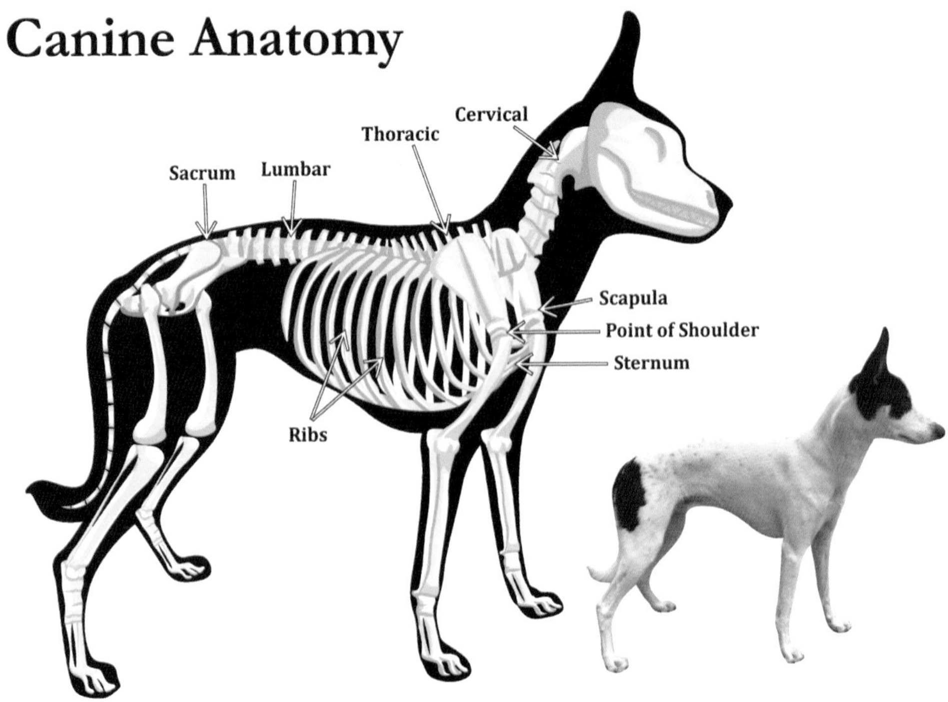


Identifying some simple bony landmarks on your dog can help you work out if your dog's harness is sitting in the right place.

Identifying these bony landmarks is a great way to get familiar with your dog's anatomy so if anything changes with harness fit, you can see where the change has occurred.

### Your Dog's Muscles

A dog's body is covered with around 700 different muscles, which hold the bony structures in place and move the dog's body; the importance of the free movement of muscles in a harness fit can't be underestimated. However, I won't be discussing muscles and muscle groups; you just need to be aware that the muscles surrounding the skeleton can affect harness fit.

Over time your dog's body can change shape too. Dogs are like humans in that they can build and lose muscle in crucial areas, which will affect the fit of a harness much in the same way that our clothes can end up not fitting if we put on, or lose weight.

If your dog is a little overweight to begin with and canicross is going to be your way to lose that weight, expect the harness to need adjusting or even replacing once you get your dog to their ideal weight. You might want to consider this in your harness selection too, as I often see dogs who have lost weight and developed muscle, who then need a different style of harness to the original choice.

## The 5-Star Harness Fitting System

### Neck

Any harness you get for your dog should leave them free to breathe easily. You shouldn't hear any wheezing or choking noises and, if you do, it is likely the harness is pulling up into the throat. This would mean the harness is having no better effect than a collar would, and you can't run a dog in a harness causing wheezing, because that means it is sitting too high on your dog's neck.

The breastbone is often used as the benchmark for harness fit. People are told the harness must sit on or below the manubrium for a correct fit but on different breeds of dogs, their breastbone is so low that if you use this as an absolute rule, then the harness will be too big overall and come down over the shoulder at the side.

The best indicator for the harness fitting correctly on the neck is to put the harness on and pull on the back of it; if the harness is sitting below the fleshy part of the throat or you can feel space at the front of the harness that you can fit a finger in, then it is probably fitting correctly on the neck.

For a correct fit on the neck, the harness doesn't need to be loose, it just needs to not restrict the breathing and one of the biggest mistakes people make when they're fitting harnesses is to have the neck too loose. If the neck is too loose then it can slip about and cause rubbing, but it can also restrict the shoulder.

The neck of your dog (unless you have a dog with a small head such as a Lurcher) will generally always be smaller than the head and you should expect any correctly fitting dog sports harness to feel snug going over your dog's head – particularly if they are a breed which has big floppy ears, such as a Spaniel. This is normal and should be expected. If your dog doesn't like tight things going over their head, you may have to put in a lot of practice, positively rewarding your dog for being calm and cooperative when putting things over their head and ears.

### Shoulder

This is probably the most important aspect of dog sports harness fit and one which is often overlooked. The dog's harness should leave the shoulder free and unrestricted to move, particularly if they are going to be pulling any weight. The harness should sit snugly in the space between the scapula and the neck. In some dogs there is a groove in the muscles to indicate where the harness would be best situated, but not all dogs will have this.

You need to assess your own dog's shoulder and decide how it needs to move to allow unrestricted movement, and then ensure the harness doesn't cover any part of the shoulder which needs to move. A simple test for this, if your dog will allow it, is to gently stretch your dog's leg forward with the harness on and if the material covers any of the shoulder which is moving forwards, then it is going to cause a restriction.

The point of the shoulder is the part of the shoulder that no part of the harness should ever cover when fitted. There are several harness designs which completely cover the shoulders, and I compare them to how it would feel to try to run in a pencil skirt. If you have material covering your legs, so that when you pull them forward, you feel resistance, then you will inevitably change the way you are moving to adjust your stride for this. The same is true of dogs.

While this would not cause a problem in the short term, any restriction or alteration of natural movement over a long period of time would cause issues with muscular health in the long term.

## Chest

When fitted correctly, the harness should not dig in behind the front legs or be too tight on the chest; the dog's leg needs to be free to move both forwards and backwards. When you do your test to see if the harness is restricting the front of the shoulder, you can also gently pull your dog's leg back (not too far) to check there is enough space behind the leg without the harness potentially rubbing there.

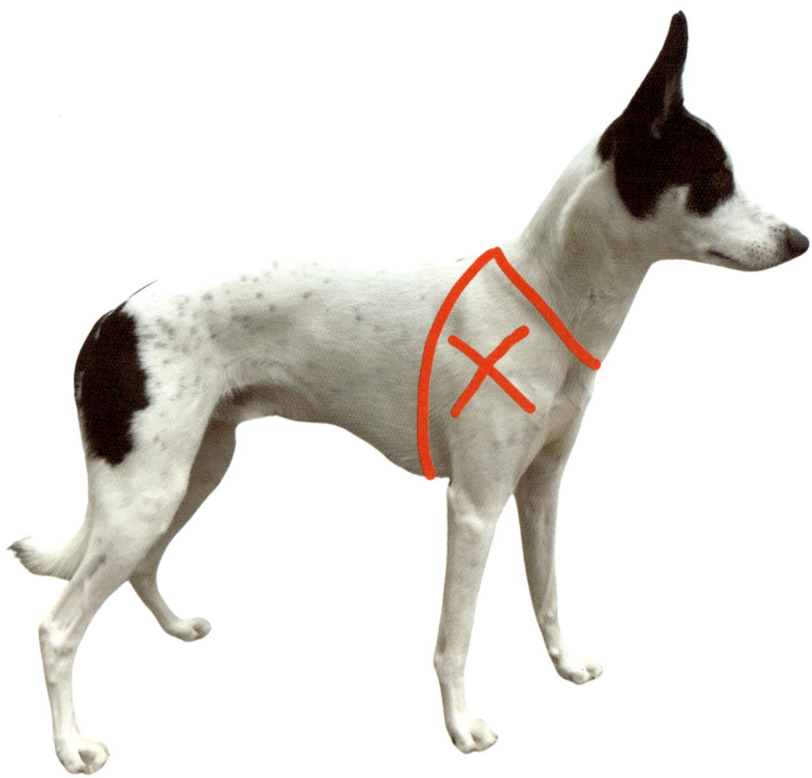

The neck of the harness should leave your dog's throat clear, but not cover up any of the large shoulder bone, which needs to be free to move.

## Ribs

The ribs end with the floating rib and so, with any style of harness, the material that comes up the side and along your dog's ribs should not be too long and come back past and beyond this last rib. If the material does come beyond this last rib, there is a risk when your dog is pulling that the harness will ride up into the soft part of your dog's stomach and put pressure on internal organs when they are running, which is not going to be comfortable for your dog.

## Hips

This will usually only apply to a longer style of harness, but could apply to a mid-length harness too. The long straps to which you attach your line should not restrict the sacrum in any way, as this is the main joint which energy transfers through your dog from their hind end to the front end, and vice versa. The whole spine needs to be able to move, and the hips act to allow the spine to flex and bend with the power generated from the back legs.

If you have a harness that puts downward pressure on the hips, then the muscles will not be able to work correctly to move your dog forwards, and there will be tension building in the muscles that operate in this area of your dog's body. So, if you are choosing a long- or mid-length harness, then you need to make sure nothing is restricting your dog's hips when they are moving. To avoid this, ensure the harness straps are not too long down the back.

It may sound like a lot, but once you get used to the bony landmarks and ensure they are all left free and unrestricted for your dog to move,

Your harness should not come behind the last ribs or restrict your dog's hips when moving.

by using the five-star harness fitting system you can check the important areas and find the best-fitting harness for your dog. It is also good to learn how to assess the fit of your dog's harness yourself, because harness fit is something which needs to be continually checked and updated, as your dog may change shape by losing weight or building muscle when they are canicrossing with you.

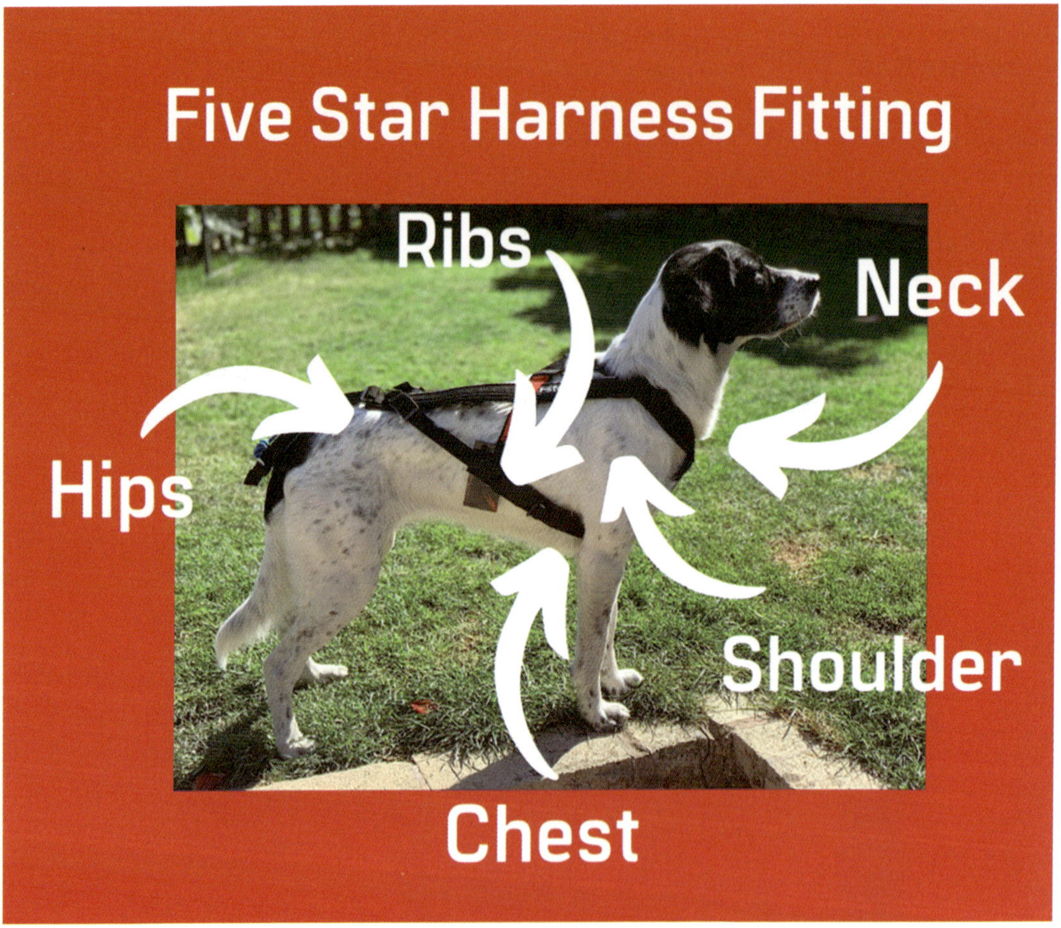


The five areas to check on your dog are the same on every dog and if you're not sure just refer to your harness supplier, who should know how to advise you.

## The Belt

The belt is an essential component of the canicross equipment, as it distributes the pulling force from the dog and protects the runner from any potential injuries. People always underestimate the importance of a canicross belt, and many people opt for a cheap line to clip around their waist, which has an integrated bungee and no sizing or padding for lower back protection. This 'strap' version of the belt isn't really a belt at all, and when people start running with a dog who pulls them, they find this strap is uncomfortable.

A proper canicross belt designed for running with your dog attached to you, will cost anywhere between about £35–£100 ($45–$128) depending on the brand and style you choose. The difference in price reflects the materials used and the time involved in production; if the belt has more adjustable parts, then it will generally be more expensive.

It is important to position the belt correctly to ensure maximum support and protection. Instead of wearing it around the waist, which can put strain on the lumbar spine, the belt should be positioned low on the hips where the force can be distributed best. The reason for this is that your hips are the strongest and most stable structure in your lower body, and provide the most surface area for any pull force to be distributed through.

Your canicross belt should always be positioned low on your body, around the widest bony structure, which is your hips.

### Features

The choice of your canicross belt depends on your individual preferences, body shape and size. There are various styles and materials available, with a wide range of prices. However, it is highly recommended to opt for a belt with leg straps. Although leg straps may feel strange at first, they play a significant role in keeping the belt in place during the physical demands of canicross, as properly fitted leg straps prevent the belt from shifting and ensure a secure and comfortable experience.

Padding is often what people will go for when they first choose a belt for canicross, but a belt that is lightweight with minimal padding can be more comfortable than one with thick padding. The most important design feature of a canicross belt should always be how it distributes any pull force from the dog on the person's body, and this can be achieved effectively through webbing straps with no padding if the design works well on the person's shape and size to do this.

You may also want to think about pockets for storage of things such as poo bags, keys and a mobile phone. Not all canicross belts will have a decent-sized pocket for storage because pockets can alter the design or fit of a belt, so you may need to think about alternative methods of storing anything you want to take on your canicross runs.

## The Bungee Line

The bungee line serves as the connection between the runner and the dog and is designed to absorb the pulling force exerted by the dog, reducing the impact on the runner's body. It is therefore important to choose a bungee line designed specifically for canicross, as generic bungee leads may not have the necessary durability and shock absorption capabilities.

Bungee lines can cost between £20–£50 ($23–$63) depending on the length and materials used. Custom lines tend to be more expensive and lines which contain longer lengths of bungee cost more to produce.

When selecting a bungee line, focus on the length of the line and its relationship to the desired level of control. If you are a beginner and prefer your dog to be closer to you, a shorter line could be more suitable. However, if your dog responds well to voice cues and you want them to be further ahead, a longer line can be used to maintain a comfortable distance for you both.

Bungee lines always get described in stretched lengths and so a 2m (2yd) bungee line will generally be around 30cm (12in) less when unstretched, giving you that 30cm (12in) of stretch to absorb the force of your dog pulling. It is recommended to check the integrity of your bungee line, including any clips, before every run, particularly if you have a dog who would be difficult to recall if they got loose. Hardware failures are thankfully rare, but the line is usually the piece of equipment that will fail first, because the bungee line is your connection and is being clipped on and off every time, creating wear on the clips.

Some bungee lines will have a clip or an integrated carabiner at both ends, and others will just have a clip or carabiner to attach to your dog and a loop to secure at the runner end. Lines with a webbing loop or handle are easily attached to the

Your bungee line length will give you more control if it's shorter and give your dog more freedom if it is longer.

Always check your bungee line is securely attached to your dog's harness, as it's your safety line and ensures your dog is connected to you.

belt by looping them through on themselves creating a secure attachment with no need for a clip, but some people prefer to have a carabiner on the belt to provide the option for quick release of your dog if you need to release them to negotiate a stile, for example.

### A Note on Race Rules

If you think you might want to race with your dog, it is worth doing a bit of research into the rules surrounding the equipment, as some race organisations do have restrictions on line length, belt width, harness style and the type of carabiner you are allowed to use – and even the use of an integral clip attaching your line to your belt. Race rules vary between race organisers and get updated with new rules from time to time, so check every event for their equipment requirements.

If you select a standard canicross line with a trigger clip or screwgate carabiner at just one end, one of the top branded belts and a harness specifically designed for dog sports, then you shouldn't have any problems.

## Running Two Dogs or More

You can run with more than one dog, and don't need to choose the same harness for each dog, as it is better to choose the harness which is right for each dog. To run with two dogs, you have a choice of two single lines, or a double line designed with two points of attachment. However, because it's not common for people to run with more than two dogs, you won't easily find lines for more than a two-dog setup.

You also need to think about whether you want to use a neckline (which is a short piece of webbing that connects two dogs by clips on their collars) or a coupler (two sections of webbing connected with a clip at the ends) to keep the dogs closer together. In my experience, the neckline is to be used for trained dogs who already run next to each other, as sometimes one of the dogs can pull the other if they are mismatched in size or ability.

Couplers or splitters give each dog a bit more space to move, but no more than a two-dog line, so if you already have a single line you're happy with, you could just add a coupler to attach another dog, particularly if you don't often run the two dogs together.

### Other Equipment to Consider

As a canicrosser, you will need to think about a few other things that will potentially be different from a normal running setup. You will mainly be running on trails and not on pavements or tarmac, so the trainers you select will need to be suitable for trail running. Running through mud is highly likely with canicross, so pay particular attention to the grip on the soles of the trainers you buy.

The discussion about the best trainers for people is as long as the information you need to know about choosing the best harness for your dog, so this book is not going to cover the range of trainers available. It is useful to know that many canicross groups and clubs will have experienced people

When running with two dogs you might want to think about using a neckline or a coupler as an additional piece of kit to keep the dogs closer together.

who can offer suggestions for brands and models of trainer, but you will need to do a bit of research for yourself when choosing your footwear.

Running clothes are also widely available with a huge range of options, and you might want to consider if you need reflective options if running at night or early in the morning in low light conditions.

You will need to decide if you have enough storage in your belt, or if you need any extra space in something like a backpack.

Running packs to carry additional items might also be on your list of considerations. Carrying a bottle of water, a collapsible dog bowl, a small first aid kit and a spare line are all recommendations I would make for anyone to have on their person when running with a dog, in case of an emergency. This is in addition to your phone, poo bags and keys.

## Frequently Asked Questions

### Can You Use Muzzles?

The short answer to this is yes, but you need to make sure that you are using a style of muzzle which allows your dog to fully open their mouth and breathe normally when exerted. Any muzzle which prevents normal panting and therefore cooling for your dog can be dangerous. Muzzles can be a valuable tool when running with a reactive dog, but their use requires careful consideration. Muzzles should never be used as a form of punishment, but rather as a safety measure for all involved. They come in various types, with wire muzzles providing space for breathing and drinking.

It's important to note that, while a muzzle can prevent a dog from causing harm to others, it doesn't eliminate the potential for fear or anxiety in your dog. Some dogs may still experience fear even if wearing a muzzle. Additionally, certain races may have rules against muzzled dogs, so be aware of event regulations.

### Coats and Fleeces

People with thin-coated dogs will sometimes add a layer onto the dog for running in cold and wet weather to keep them comfortable when they are not moving fast on runs. If you do put a coat or fleece on your dog to keep them warm, you need to be extra vigilant to ensure they are not overheating, and you should check your dog regularly to make sure they are not too warm from the heat generated through exercise. It is generally better to use coats and fleeces for keeping your dog's muscles warm before or after runs, as human athletes do.

### Cooling Jackets

The use of cooling jackets for running is not advised, although many of the manufacturers will advertise their products as being suitable for this type of use. It could be very dangerous if your dog is being run in warmer weather with something over them that prevents their own natural cooling functions. Cooling jackets will usually work through the evaporative effect of water, and as soon as the jacket begins to dry out it turns into a regular jacket which traps heat in. It is safer to assume that if your dog is going to be warm enough to need a cooling coat, then it is too warm to be running your dog and leave the run for another, cooler day.

### Boots

Boots for paw protection can be useful if your dog has softer pads, or has dry or cracked pads which can damage easily, or if you know your dog is going to have to run on sections of trail which are more likely to cause pad injury.

There are many different styles and brands of dog boots now, and you might want to have some handy just in case, but in general it is advisable not to run your dog consistently in boots due to the potential for overheating. Dogs lose heat through their paws and, if covered by boots, your dog loses one of their natural ways to keep cool. It is better to leave their feet free of material to allow more natural movement and function.

There are a range of boots you can buy now for dogs; you need to decide if you need the paw protection for your dog and if they will allow your dog's paws to move naturally.

Running with your dog will feel effortless once you find the right equipment and have it fitted correctly for you both.

Choose your canicross belt based on your requirements and what feels comfortable for you.

## SUMMARY

Although choosing the correct harness and equipment for running with your dog can seem like a daunting task, just remember the basics:

- Dog sports harnesses are specifically designed for the task of pulling.
- The harness should be lightweight and water-resistant.
- Choose a harness based on your dog's body shape and pulling style.
- Don't be afraid to try something new or different from the most popular brand.
- Short harnesses suit more leisurely pullers.
- Long harnesses suit strong pullers.
- If your dog is of a stockier, shorter-backed breed and a strong puller, try a mid-length harness.
- Belts are better with leg straps and can be chosen for your comfort.
- Bungee lines are all designed to absorb pull; choose your length based on the level of control you need (shorter = more control).
- Other considerations for kit to run with your dog are all based around the safety and comfort of you and your dog.

Once you know you want to give canicross a try, you need to think about how to get started on training with your dog in a way that will work best for you.

# CHAPTER 3
# How to Canicross

Canicross, as we know, is not simply running with your dog, as some people will suggest – although it is one of the most accessible dog sports, because you don't need to be in a specific venue to take part. You will need to do some training for the sport, and I have seen and heard of people who decided to give canicross a try without the right equipment or any training, who have not enjoyed their experience. It is important to get started the right way, and if you take some time to incorporate proper canicross training into your life, then you will have the most fun.

You can start up on your own, just you and your dog, with your belt, bungee lead and dog sport harness, as described in the previous chapter. You might want some guidance from something like the NHS Couch to 5km (3mi) app, and you will need to focus on the training, which will be discussed in this chapter.

If you are interested in getting a bit more support to get started, you might want to find a social canicross group in your area; many are listed on canicross websites as a free resource to access, and are a great way to connect with like-minded people who enjoy the sport. Social groups will often have kit bags, and this is a sensible solution to get started and try the kit that works best for you without having to pay money up front. Running with other dogs in a group can also be the quickest way your dog learns what is expected of them too.

Canicross clubs are usually social groups who have taken the steps to become more formally recognised and set up as a proper club. Canicross clubs will almost always have a kit bag that you can access and also have insurance, which covers you for any third-party liability when you are running with them on an organised run.

Canicrossing with others in a group or in a club can give you access to training tips and different options of equipment to try.

## A Note on Insurance

Third-party insurance is something you can look at getting as an individual for canicross and is something you will need to check, as some pet insurance policies do not cover your dog while they are canicrossing. If you want to race, you will need individual third-party liability cover for any injury you and your dog might cause a member of the public, regardless of the race organisers insurance.

## Canicross Coaches

There are now a number of canicross coaches across the UK who are training people to canicross in classes, much the same as a personal trainer or a running club. Finding a reputable coach can be a fantastic way to get started with your dog if you are unsure or nervous about starting on your own.

Do make sure you do your due diligence on your trainer, asking them what their experience is, have they ever raced, how many dogs do they own/run with and how many dogs have they trained to canicross. All these questions might seem obvious, but sometimes running coaches expand into canicross without any solid knowledge of the dog training that goes into the sport, and it is very important to have a canicross coach who knows the elements of dog health, as well as safety considerations for dog owners.

Canicross coaches can provide you with extra structure for your runs and spend time with you specifically training your voice cues to make your canicrossing safer.

## Warming Up and Cooling Down

Just as we are taught to warm up and cool down for running, it is important to also warm up and cool down your dog, for all the same reasons. It is a fairly new concept in canicross to warm up and cool down and so if you join a group, you may find that members don't incorporate this into their runs. If you find this, make sure you allow yourself some extra time before you meet up with the others to do this as part of your routine.

## Warming Up

You will be helping to prevent injury in your dog and prolong their active life by completing a few simple exercises before you start your runs. Here are some suggestions for a warm-up:

***Brisk walking*:** begin at a slow pace, then get faster so your dog is warming up the muscles slowly when you get them out of the car. You can turn this into a slow jog to get your dog's (and your own) heart rate up, to encourage blood flow and prepare you for running.

***Weave in different directions*:** when walking, get your dog to move in different directions, around natural obstacles if there are any (that is, a big stone or puddle), or set out your own markers on the ground. This will activate side stretches for your dog and prepare them for any turns when running.

Brisk walking is a simple, yet effective, way to warm up your dog and should be done before every run to ensure your dog's muscles are getting warmer and their heart rate is elevated.

*Circles*: walking your dog in a bigger circle, decreasing the circle in size on repetitions can help to activate the muscles along the side of your dog to prepare them for any turns. Stick to only a few circles in both directions so you don't get dizzy.
*Figures-of-eight*: another useful walking exercise to activate muscles in preparation for running; all of these give you the opportunity to practise your directional voice cues before your run too.

#### Hands-on Muscle Warm-up

*Pre-run massage*: use this to create surface warmth in the muscles to bring the blood to the surface of the skin. Imagine you are rubbing hand cream into your dog's coat for your technique. With an excitable dog, use slow strokes and for a calm dog use faster strokes. Use a combination of both short and long strokes. Start at the neck and move between the chest, down the outside of each leg and up the inside of the leg, taking care around the groin area and checking for any areas of discomfort. Ideally, this should be without the harness on, but can be done with the harness on if you need to.

#### Additional Muscle Activation Exercises

*Pad touching*: give your dog a quick proprioceptive workout by touching each pad and stimulating their feet in preparation for exercise.
*Sit to stand*: this activates your dog's core and hind limbs ready for powering forwards when canicrossing.
*Sit, wait and recall to you*: this can be done off lead if you have the recall or on lead if not, activating the muscles which drive your dog forwards and preparing them for action.
*Stand to down or bow*: this will activate muscles to engage and prepare your dog for running; don't make the stretches too long, and allow your dog to complete these to their own comfort.

Simple and short will be enough to warm your dog up.

Simple dynamic movement exercises to encourage your dog to activate muscles they are going to use during canicross will also help your dog to warm up.

### Cooling Down

The aim of your cool-down is to decrease your dog's heart rate gradually, so slow your speed down during the last part of your run – very similar to the warm-up with jogging, decreasing to a brisk walk and back down into a slow walk; don't just run to the finish and stop.

Everything you have done for your warm-up can be done in reverse to cool down, so weaving in different directions, circles and figures of eight can all be done with turns that increase in size and slow in pace.

Gently rub your dog's muscles down using light, soft strokes to calm and cool your dog, but remember if you do too much of this, you will not be allowing your dog to cool down as the strokes will generate heat.

***Neck and body stretches:*** train your dog to drop their head down between their front legs and then around to each side, as far as they are comfortable. Do not force your dog to stretch beyond what they offer you. This will encourage a natural flexion without overstretching muscles at the end of a run.

Always make sure that if the weather is warmer you have plenty of water and a cool space for your dog to relax after canicrossing. If the weather is cold, you should have a warm, dry blanket for them to lie on and don't leave anything wet or muddy on them. If you have a fleece coat, then this is ideal if your dog needs something extra to keep them warm following exercise.

## WARMING UP AND COOLING DOWN

The importance of a warm-up and cool-down is imperative for the longevity of your dog in any dog sport. It is advisable to tailor your exercises under the supervision of a qualified veterinary physiotherapist to ensure your dog's canicross programme meets their individual needs within their physical capabilities, taking account of any strengths and weaknesses.

Tace Allen, Veterinary Physiotherapist

Starting your canicrossing in a social group can be fun and give you the motivation you need to get out and do the training.

## Before You Start

### Toileting and Your Training

If you want your dog to run consistently, then you need to ensure that you have taken your dog to the toilet first or make specific stops for their comfort.

Do make sure you're not running in front of your dog; you don't want to be teaching them to follow you. Ideally, give them the cues and get them out in front of you right from the outset, so there's no confusion later on in your training.

### Rest

As with any new training you do with your dog, keep your training short to begin with, don't do too much, too soon, and always make sure you finish your sessions with your dog wanting to do more, not exhausted from the effort.

Factor in plenty of rest days; dogs need to recover from physical effort, and giving your dog breaks from training allows them to process what they have learned.

## Training Your Voice Cues

Voice cues are a huge part of canicross training and the time you put into this should be prioritised. After many years of canicrossing I still take time to work on training my voice cues, because they are your main form of communication with your dog.

The choice of the cues you train are down to you, but there is a list of suggested cues below. If the actual words don't resonate with you, then use a word which does. It doesn't matter what the cue word is, as long as you are consistent with your word and how you train it. For example, some old-school mushing terms are:

'Gee', which means turn right.
'Haw', which means turn left.
'Hike on', which means pull forward.
'On by', which means carry straight on.

These words may mean nothing to you, so feel free to choose your own set of cues. Use whatever will be easiest for you to train your dog with.

## Your Main Canicross Cues

### Pull

A pull cue is a cue to encourage your dog out in front of you and to pull into the harness. The reason for training a pull cue for canicross dogs is that if you train your dog to pull, then you can also train them not to pull. Giving them a cue to let your dog know they are allowed to pull not only helps with the difference between canicross training and normal on-lead walk training, but means you can indicate to your dog when they are allowed to pull and train it to make it fun.

### Line Out

A line out cue is used to get your dog to stand quietly and calmly at the end of the bungee line, waiting for the next cue to go. The purpose of training a line out cue is to prevent your dog dragging you around, bouncing around excited on the end of your bungee line, when they know they are going to be running. Canicross is fun but if you teach a calm line out cue, your dog will learn they have to start running in a controlled way, to prevent both of you from getting injured by starting off too quickly.

Teaching your dog to line out can take some time and patience, but it can be very useful to have your dog calm and waiting for your cue to run.

## Directions

Your directional cues (your left and right) are what you will be using to guide your dog on the trails when you are running. Training clear direction cues will help you move quickly away from something you want to avoid, or just move in the direction you want in an uninterrupted way.

## Steady

Training a steady cue is one for safety, to get your dog to slow down in front of you when you come across something which might cause you a problem; for example a steep hill or any uneven, rutted ground. When you use your steady cue, you will be able to negotiate hazards with your dog effortlessly and not get pulled over.

## Straight on

Your straight on cue is one that gives your dog the instruction they need to keep moving forward in a straight line and not get distracted by other paths on the trail, other users, wildlife or other distracting smells or sights. You can use a straight on cue to get past obstacles and indicate to your dog not to turn or slow down.

## Back or Behind

The back or behind cue can also be 'in close' or 'heel', because it gets your dog to come in close or behind you to ensure they are not out front pulling you at that particular point in your run. You can use this cue in many different situations if you come to a hazard, such as a road or a particularly steep downhill where you should be in front. You can also use this cue to protect your dog from anything they might be scared of, putting yourself between them and the perceived danger, giving them more confidence in you.

## Stop

The stop cue is an emergency cue to get your dog to stop instantly, or just to stop moving if they are trying to move off when you don't want them to. The stop cue is a good one for unexpected hazards appearing in front of you, or if something happens which requires you to stop, such as your shoelaces coming undone.

## Over

The over cue is used in conjunction with a direction cue to ask your dog to move over on a path, but not actually turn in that direction. Over cues can be used to move around obstacles in the way and, if you eventually get racing with your canicross dog, you can use an over cue for overtaking or being overtaken safely.

Training your dog to run beside or behind you can be useful in many situations, including if you want to protect your dog, and is a cue you can start training from a young age.

## How to Train Your Voice Cues

The main thing to remember when training your dog to respond to your voice cues is to try to shape the behaviour to happen, and then cue the behaviour as it happens. So, when your dog is turning right, call 'right' then praise and reward them. Your dog will learn that turning right is associated with the word 'right' and then you can begin to call the cue before you get to the turn.

Another example is to encourage your dog behind you or beside you by guiding your line backwards on a narrow trail so they can't get around you – and when they are in the position you want, call the cue then praise and reward your dog.

### Praise and Reward

This is the key to training your voice cues effectively. You might just use verbal praise, you might give a few small treats, or you might use a physical reward, such as a head stroke, or let them carry a favourite toy for a short time. Whatever rewards your dog best, use that for the strongest response to training, and remember you can reinforce your voice cues in all sorts of circumstances, at home and on walks if you are consistent.

Don't change your words when you are training voice cues; keep everything simple for your dog to understand. By making training consistent and simple, you will get better results, faster.

Whatever your voice cue is for the behaviour, try to only reinforce it once – don't keep repeating the cue over and over, or add in extra words so your dog starts to switch off to the cue. The best voice cues are simple words, issued once, and then not repeated until the next time they are needed.

### Set Your Dog Up to Win

Practise your voice cues around obstacles you have on your runs, using natural landmarks to mark points for your dog to run to or run around, and don't make things harder for your dog than you need to. Running across an open field and calling a direction is going to make that turn much harder for your dog to achieve than if you take them on a narrow trail with only a left turn, and call the cue as you turn left. They can't fail to get that correct, so you set them up to win. You can also use things such as gates to train your steady cue. Your dog will naturally slow down on approach to a gate or stile, so use this opportunity to issue your 'steady' voice cue and your dog will be successful.

Giving your dog a clearly defined path with few other options when training sets your dog up for success and means you can reward them for simply doing what you have guided them to do.

## Techniques for Canicross Running

There are certain little tricks for running with your dog that work for canicrossing. If you're asking your dog to run uphill, pump your own arms, raise your own knees and look towards where you are going to encourage your dog to keep running too.

If you are running downhill with your dog, the most natural thing to do is to lean back and brace yourself against your dog, but if you lean forwards and go with your dog, you will find this an easier (and less painful) downhill running technique. Look up at where you are going and not down at your feet.

If you are running over uneven ground, try to keep as light on your feet as you can, as the less volume of foot on the ground, the less likely you are to become unbalanced and go over on an ankle.

General running form is to keep your head high, your shoulders and your arms relaxed and not hunched up. Try not to sag through your waist and keep as light on your feet as you can, with a high knee action.

Running with a dog can be very different from normal running. The extra pull can make you 'overstride' where you are pulled further in the air than you would be naturally, which tends to result in a heavier landing and more strain on your body, so do keep this in mind when you first start canicrossing.

Even if you are an experienced runner, canicross can be quite a different physical sport and the demands on your body usually leave you with sore muscles on the first attempt as you recruit new, previously unused muscles.

Good running form, keeping your body upright but relaxed and keeping light on your feet, rather than bracing against your dog when canicrossing, can help you avoid injury.

## Ladder Training

Think about the training as rungs on a ladder and, if you get stuck at any point, just drop back down the ladder rungs until you start to see progress again. The first rung on the ladder might be a short distance of out front pulling 100–500m (110–547yd) on single track paths, teaching your line out.

The second rung on the ladder might be teaching your directional cues: right, left and straight on.

The third rung on the ladder may be more complex voice cues or short distances of running out front pulling 100–500m (110–547yd) in wider, more open, spaces.

The fourth rung on the ladder could include short distances of running with changes of direction, increasing the distance of the runs to up to 1km (⅔mi), ensuring your dog is happy to keep in front the whole time. Your ladder rungs will involve continually increasing the distance to your own training plan, using the skills you are learning. Keep progressing until you feel confident covering longer distances, and using your voice cues to effectively communicate with your dog for fun running.

If you have any problems in your training, go back a couple of steps, take a breather and start again; canicrossing can take time to train for both of you.

## SUMMARY

- You can start your canicross training in a number of different ways.
- Warming up and cooling down should be part of every training session.
- Voice cues should be kept simple and clear.
- Positive associations with your training will ensure your dog enjoys the sport.
- If you encounter any problems, take a few steps back until you and your dog are confident again.

The environment you canicross in is important to consider for you and your dog's comfort and safety.

# CHAPTER 4
# The Canicross Environment

Once you have the equipment and an idea of the training involved in canicross, you will probably start to think about the different places you can take your dog canicrossing. It can be fun to explore your local area and even further afield as part of the experience. There are a few things you will need to consider before you venture out with your dog, to keep you both happy and safe.

## Accessibility

Canicross is a sport easily accessible to everyone, and you can take your dog from your doorstep to run with you, which is one of things that makes it so popular. There are very few sports that do not require a particular venue or have such a wide variety of terrains suitable for the sport as canicross, but just because you can run with your dog anywhere, doesn't mean you necessarily should

## Terrain

You may have heard people talking about the impact of road running on the human body, and although dogs, being quadrupeds, are much more efficient runners than we are, there are still considerations for running your dog on certain types of terrain.

While a dog won't suffer the same impact injuries as a person running on hard surfaces because the weight is distributed through four limbs rather than two, you still need to think about the damage to your dog's pads that may occur from harsher surfaces. Tarmac, flinty trails and anything with a hard, sharp or uneven construction can cause a problem for a dog's softer pads, whereas we have the protection of our trainers.

For your dog, it is preferable to plan your canicross runs on trails. Grass or woodland tracks are the least likely to cause pad or paw issues, so try to stick to softer paths for the majority of your route. These types of tracks will be better for your dog and, although a little bit of road running is fine, you need to think about your joints, and those of your dog, over the longer term. You will probably both enjoy running more in rural areas, with nature around you, where you can benefit fully from the outdoor experience. Urban running in built-up areas can present more hazards and, particularly when beginning your training, can make it difficult to concentrate on your dog if you are looking out for people and traffic.

For canicross it is better for you and your dog to find softer, more interesting, trails to run on, rather than running on roads.

## The Canicross Season

It has already been mentioned that the canicross season in the UK generally runs from September to April or May. This avoids having any 'in season' races during the supposedly warmer months of June, July and August. Often there is plenty of opportunity for canicross in these months, as the British weather is well known for being changeable. What is important to observe is how your dog responds to the warmer weather and what temperatures they can cope with. Regardless of what anyone else is doing with their dog, you have to be considerate of the individual heat tolerance of your own dog and make your canicross environment fit around this.

For example, if your dog doesn't cope well with warmer weather, then include lots of natural water stops on your route, being aware of hazards such as blue-green algae and other problems with potentially contaminated water sources. If your dog doesn't cope well in the cold, then ensure your route isn't open to the wind and rain, running in more sheltered areas to protect your dog better from the elements. Wherever you are in the world, you will need to be mindful of seasonal temperature changes and what your dog is acclimatised to, so that you can plan your own canicross season which is suitable and safe for running in.

Finding trails with natural water incorporated in them is better in the warmer weather to ensure your dog will have the chance to cool down.

## A Good Canicross Environment

A good canicross environment is one which caters nicely for your dog's needs and provides an interesting and safe route for you both to run in. If you are worrying about hazards on the route, then it won't be as enjoyable and canicross should always be about fun and having a positive experience.

First, if you're running from home then you don't need to worry about having a toilet at your destination; you can make sure you and your dog have had your pre-run comfort breaks in the confines of your own property. However, if you are driving any distance to your run route, then you might want to consider if the venue has a toilet for you and a toilet area for your dog.

The parking should be safe and secure for you to be able to get your dog out of the car and harnessed up without worrying about oncoming traffic. A big open car park is ideal, but if this isn't possible then at least somewhere you have enough space that you can manage your dog's needs safely.

Your route should start out with a flat and simple terrain so you can complete your warm-up effectively before you move into more technical single-track trail or hilly areas. It is also worth

Start your canicross runs on flat, even and straightforward terrain to allow you and your dog to warm up properly and avoid injury when you are both starting out.

remembering that if you have a keen dog, a steep decline in the first kilometre might not be the most sensible option and it is better to keep steep inclines or declines to the middle or end of your run route when you and your dog are warmed up, focused and less likely to get injured.

## Other Environmental Factors

If you are running through fields, make sure there aren't going to be problems with livestock that might affect you or your dog's confidence. Running through herds of farm animals can be dangerous and so, if possible, avoid fields regularly used for cattle, horses and sheep.

Some fields can also have steep off-camber sections, which can put a lot of strain on one side of your body to enable balance, so if you are new to running on trails and haven't experienced running off-camber, then keep this to a minimum while you build up strength, balance and flexibility to avoid injury.

If you are lucky enough to run through woodland, tracks with lots of tree roots can be tiring to run on, as your concentration is focused on looking at your feet, so make sure your skill level in canicross matches the technical element of the terrain you are running on, and keep things simple to begin with.

Natural sources of water are always a benefit on any canicross run route, giving you a chance to catch your breath and your dog a chance to take a little drink. You can, of course, carry water for you and your dog, but sometimes the cooling effect of running water that your dog can dip their body into can't be matched. Plus, even if your dog doesn't like water, the variety in routes with natural water stops makes everything more interesting in terms of sights, smells and sounds.

Canicross routes with plenty of natural shade are also a bonus; they not only protect you from the sun if it's warm, but also the rain and wind when it is cold.

A good idea when planning canicross routes is to try to incorporate shortcuts, so that if anything were to happen, either to yourself or your dog, then you have a way to cut your run short and get back home, or to your car quickly if you need to. It might not always be possible, but having knowledge of any shortcuts can help in the case of a problem.

Woodland trails can be lots of fun for canicrossing, but make sure when you are starting out that there aren't too many tree roots to provide trip hazards for you.

## A Bad Canicross Environment

The type of canicross environment unsuitable for running with your dog are routes that have a lot of tarmac, hard, flinty, or very sharp-surfaced trails. Anything that could cause damage to your dog's pads is something to be avoided.

Urban canicross is something you can do with your dog, and short stretches of pavement or tarmac are fine, but you also need to think about what is going to be most stimulating for your dog. They will almost certainly prefer softer trails and an environment with different smells and surfaces, so keeping your road running to a minimum is better for your dog's physical health, mental health and safety.

You don't want to be running with your dog next to busy roads or on paths where you meet a lot of other people. Particularly when you are starting out, having lots of hazards and distractions can be very off-putting, so choose trails where there is less footfall, making sure you're setting your dog up for success with their training.

Depending on the time of day you are canicrossing, however, you might not want the trails to be too isolated, and for your safety, when running at night or in the early morning, this might mean choosing paths which are better known and have more people using them.

Safety must be at the forefront of your mind for both you and your dog when canicrossing. If you are on your own, it is always worth telling someone where you are going and possibly adding an app on your phone so your chosen contact could find you in case of an emergency.

Choose your routes carefully to make sure you are comfortable where you are running. You might feel safer having your dog with you, but there may still be places you are better avoiding at night or in the early morning. If you

Choosing less busy trails with few distractions can allow you to focus on your training with your dog, particularly when you are beginners to the sport.

do have to canicross in the dark, you can always use head torches, dog lights, reflective running gear and even reflective covers to highlight yourself to other trail users and make yourself more visible.

## Seeking Permission to Canicross

Most places you can canicross will not require permission for you to use the trails. That is one of the best things about the sport and makes it so accessible for everyone. Footpaths, bridleways, shared access cycleways, many forests, parks and open access areas welcome considerate walkers and trail users.

If you are canicrossing, you will have your dog under control and so you might find you are more welcome to use the land than other dog walkers, because your dog will not be able to disturb wildlife and you will pick up after your dog if they toilet in fields or on paths, which other dog owners might not do.

The only time that seeking permission becomes more important is when you are in an organised group. Some forestry commissions and national parks require permits when you are meeting up in larger groups, and even if it is just a social run, be mindful that a group of people running with their dogs can be quite intimidating. Landowners might be more wary about having groups meeting up in parks or woods if they are concerned about public liability.

Not everyone understands canicross and it can be seen as something similar to sled dog or Greyhound racing by people who don't know any better. Remember to explain to people that you meet out and about, while it is a sport, it's just running with your dog attached and we train for it, so we have fun and are in control.

If you do find yourself wondering if you need to ask permission, then it is probably best to find out who to approach and ask the question, to avoid any misunderstanding. Most landowners will happily grant you this when you explain what you do, and it is better to build positive relationships with people in your local area than cause tension through a lack of communication.

Canicrossing in a bigger group can draw attention to the sport and it might be worth checking with the landowner that they are happy for you to use the space for group runs.

## SUMMARY

- You can run with your dog anywhere you can walk with your dog.
- You do need to be aware of the terrain you are running on for the general health and welfare of your dog.
- Consider the safety aspect of your runs, especially if you are running on your own.
- Be aware of the impact of warmer or cooler weather, uneven trails, livestock and other trail users when choosing your routes.
- If you are running in a group, do make sure you have the landowners' permission to be there.

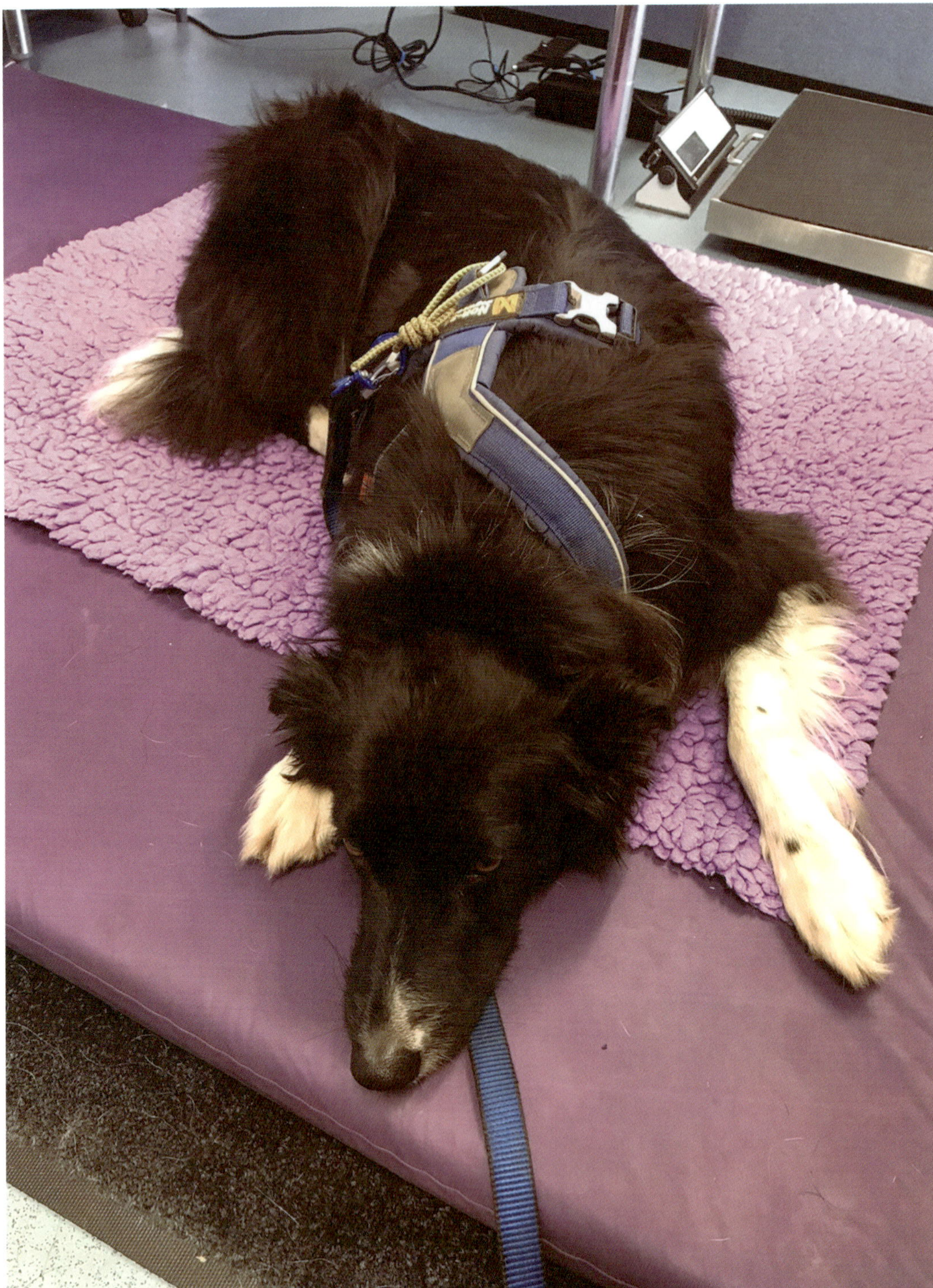

Considering the health of yourself and your dog, and consulting with professionals before you start running together, is important to prevent any problems occurring.

# CHAPTER 5
# Health Considerations

Canicross is something already discussed as being beneficial for the physical and mental health of both you and your dog, but many people feel that a particular health condition might prevent them from even considering taking part in canicross or canihiking.

It is always sensible to make carefully considered choices when deciding if canicross is going to be suitable for you as a team, and it is advisable to seek either a medical or veterinary consultation if you're not sure if the increased activity will be detrimental. However, having seen many people and dogs who have overcome physical and mental challenges, then go on to enjoy many years of fun within the sport, I would suggest that with adaptions, canicross can be a way to support some of the more common medical or veterinary conditions. By the end of this chapter, you will see the range of conditions canicrossers have experienced and shaped the sport for.

## Observation

One of the most important things I advise dog owners to do when they first start canicrossing is to observe their dog to understand their dog's 'normal'. This is crucial in being able to identify when your dog is moving and behaving normally and when they are not.

You are the one who knows your dog best, and therefore you are the person who should start this process of understanding your dog before they begin canicross. The reason for this is to have a base line for your dog before beginning a new exercise regime, that is recorded and monitored, so you can understand if anything has changed with the introduction of canicross to your routine.

### Vital Signs

In the same way that we look at our own vital signs to indicate health, we also need to be checking the vital signs of our dogs. At a minimum, know your dog's resting heart rate, respiratory rate and temperature.

A dog's resting heart rate should be between 60–120 beats per minute, with fitter dogs often having rates at the lower end of the scale, regardless of the dog's size or breed. The easiest way to check your dog's heart rate is to put your hand on the inside of the rear leg at mid-thigh. You should feel the femoral artery pulsing near the surface, although this can be difficult to find with some breeds; it can be easier to find if your dog is standing. Count the number of beats you feel during a 15-second period and multiply by four to get the beats per minute.

A dog's resting respiratory rate should be between 15 and 30 breaths per minute and the easiest way to take this is to watch your dog's chest rise and fall for 30 seconds when they are resting or asleep and multiply by two the number of breaths they take during your observations.

A dog's normal internal body temperature should between 38.3–39.3°C, but your dog may be slightly outside of this range as their normal. Your dog probably won't thank you for taking their temperature, as the easiest way is a lubricated thermometer in their rectum, and if you don't feel comfortable doing this yourself at home, then ask your vet to do this the next time your dog has a check-up, so you can get an idea of what is normal.

These vital signs are useful for you to monitor your dog's health and fitness to understand when you need to stop because they are not recovering quickly, or have a significant change in any of these vital signs following exercise.

Observing your dog before, during and after canicross is an important part of making sure you keep your dog safe and notice any changes in their movement or behaviour.

Taking the time to monitor your dog's respiratory rate when resting allows you to understand when they are working hard while exercising, and therefore not push them too hard.

## Other Things to Monitor

You should monitor your dog's weight throughout their lives and if you don't have access to weighing scales regularly, use a body condition score chart, which is based on the way your dog looks and feels when you run soft hands over their back, ribs and hips. Be aware of any weight loss, weight gain and the overall condition of your dog, so they are not losing weight through the increase in exercise, and not gaining weight if you are upping their food to fuel the new activity.

Any changes to your dog's skin or coat can be an indication of a problem in their muscles or in their overall health, so don't ignore any such changes that you might observe.

Monitoring your dog's paws and claws is important, particularly if you have to run on harder ground, which may cause damage to your dog's pads or wear down the claws more quickly. Keeping the claws trimmed short will also ensure your dog isn't having to move abnormally to compensate for long claws.

The importance of making sure your dog is a suitable age for canicross has already been discussed, but it is worth mentioning again here as a health factor that you need to consider. A younger dog or an older dog might need more closely monitoring than a dog considered in their 'prime' of life, so when you are doing your observations, include age as an influencing factor.

## Common Canine Conditions

When engaging in canicross, it is crucial to consider your dog's overall health and any existing medical conditions. The first thing to do in making sure your dog is fit for the sport, is always to consult with your veterinarian to ensure the safety and well-being of your dog.

Additionally, it is worth checking your pet insurance policy for what they will cover your dog for when taking part in canicross, as individual insurance policy coverage for sports-related activities may vary.

### Arthritis

Arthritis is often a concern for dog owners considering canicross. However, with proper management and guidance from your vet, it may still be possible for arthritic dogs to participate. While arthritis may require a more gentle pace and careful monitoring, controlled exercise like canicross can help maintain muscle strength and joint mobility. Consult with your vet to determine the suitability and limitations for your dog.

### Heart Conditions

If your dog has a heart condition, it is vital to consult with a veterinary cardiologist to assess their specific situation. In some cases, exercise can be beneficial for the heart muscle. However, individualised guidance is essential to ensure your dog's safety. Cardiologists can provide recommendations on appropriate exercise levels and any necessary precautions.

### Orthopaedic Conditions

Dogs diagnosed with orthopaedic conditions such as elbow or hip dysplasia can still participate in canicross with proper supervision and veterinary input. Controlled canicross can aid in building muscle strength and supporting joint stability. Consult with your vet to determine the stage and severity of the condition and seek guidance on managing your dog's participation.

## Case Study: Hattie

Jo was disheartened to learn that her very active Labrador, Hattie, needed an operation after a diagnosis of severe elbow dysplasia and mild hip dysplasia. Jo wasn't sure what exercise Hattie was going to be able to do, being diagnosed at such a young age, but has worked with her vets and physiotherapist to tailor a training program that will support Hattie's conditions. The professional feedback has been that Hattie is able to do more now at six years old, because she had the opportunity to build up muscle in the controlled way that canicross allows.

Hattie has been able to keep fit and active following her elbow and hip dysplasia diagnosis. Both the vet and physiotherapist have agreed canicross has been beneficial for her.

## Epilepsy

For dogs with epilepsy, it is crucial to identify and understand their specific triggers. If exercise-related triggers are not present, canicross may be suitable. However, always consult your vet to ensure the condition is well-managed and that the activity will not worsen their epilepsy. Remember, individual cases may vary, and veterinary advice is paramount.

## Addison's Disease

Addison's disease, a condition affecting the adrenal glands, does not necessarily mean the end of your dog's active life. With proper management and guidance from your vet, dogs with Addison's disease can continue to participate in canicross. It is essential to establish a comprehensive management plan to ensure their well-being and closely monitor their condition.

## Blind Dogs

As already touched on, blind dogs can take part in canicross.You will need to make sure your dog is happy to be guided by your voice cues, and you will need to take particular care to make sure that you never let anything negative happen to your dog while canicrossing, so they continue to trust you as their guide.

## Deaf Dogs

Deaf dogs can also take part in canicross; you just need to adapt your cues when you train, to cater for the fact that you will not be able to use the traditional voice cues. You might need to adapt hand signals or taps on your dog's bungee line to communicate with your dog.

## Tri-pawed Dogs

Dogs who are missing a leg are also capable of canicrossing. It may be harder to find a harness to fit properly if your dog is missing a forelimb, but people have usually been able to find something suitable with the guidance of an experienced retailer. The other main consideration with a tri-pawed dog is the maintenance and support of the remaining limbs, so they are not overused, causing muscle tightness or pain. So, if you want to run with a three-legged dog, it's recommended that you invest in a good physiotherapist and take their advice on how to protect your dog from any injury.

### Case Study: Juno

Angelica discovered Juno was losing her sight through incidents of injury and difficulty seeing toys and obstacles. She was eventually diagnosed with progressive retinal atrophy and one day lost her sight completely. After Juno went fully blind, Angelica continued canicross training, using her verbal cues instead of visual ones. She has found that Juno trusts her to guide her running, and the only additional cues she has taught Juno is to step up and step down. Anjelica has also invested in some specific canine goggles to protect Juno's eyes from injury and allow her to keep enjoying her running safely. Anjelica has found that Juno only runs properly now when she is attached in her canicross kit, because it gives her confidence knowing that Anjelica will give her the cues she needs.

## Consultation with Your Vet

The examples provided above are not exhaustive, but they highlight the importance of consulting with your vet about any medical condition your dog may have. Each dog is unique, and their specific medical needs should be considered before engaging in canicross. Your vet can provide the most accurate guidance based on your dog's individual circumstances, ensuring their safety and enjoyment.

### THE IMPORTANCE OF KEEPING FIT

Keeping dogs fit, active and moving benefits both their physical and mental health. Joints need movement to keep them healthy, and canicross and canihiking can be a great way to do this for many dogs with long-term health conditions. Always ensure your pet is assessed by your vet and a qualified musculoskeletal therapist before commencing, and then monitor regularly to ensure they are still fit and safe to compete.

Rachel Mowbray-Richardson BVSc MRCVS, CCRP, Director, The Renew Centre

## Human Health Considerations

Individuals with medical conditions should consult their doctor before starting canicross. Whether you have a heart condition, autoimmune disorder, orthopaedic issue, epilepsy or any other concern, it is essential to seek medical advice before engaging in a new activity. Certain conditions may require adjustments or considerations, such as medications that can be affected by exercise.

In cases where there is a medical concern, carrying a card or identification specifying your condition and required treatments can be beneficial, especially when participating in more isolated areas. It is equally important to carry any necessary medications or allergy treatments if you are prone to allergies that might be encountered while canicrossing.

### Allergies

People with allergies, particularly severe reactions to bee or wasp stings, should be prepared and carry necessary medications like EpiPens while canicrossing. Since canicross often takes place in more remote or isolated areas, it is crucial to have the means to manage allergic reactions if they occur. Ensuring that others are aware of your medical condition and having the appropriate measures readily available can be life-saving in case of an emergency.

## Disabilities

Canicrossing with a disability can be challenging but not impossible, and there are many people who have managed to adapt the sport to allow them to take part safely. For example, it might seem prohibitive for people who use a wheelchair for mobility to take part in this sport, which is centred around running with dogs. However, where there is a will, there is usually a way, and with the power of social media it is possible to get information and help for anyone who has a physical disability to get equipment to attach their dog to their wheelchair or mobility scooter to allow them to participate.

Hidden disabilities can also be catered for with canicross, and many people have reported how canicross has helped them to overcome their own anxieties and live active lives with their dog. Canicrossers can train their existing assistance dogs to run with them as an additional way to bond and enjoy activity together.

### ASSISTANCE DOGS AND CANICROSS

My main experience has been about experimentation. There is no kit out there available for wheelchairs like there is for bikes and scooters, so the best thing I can recommend is trying as many different bits of equipment as you can get your hands on to see what works best. But also, don't be afraid to say something just doesn't work out. My biggest recommendation for people is to search for online groups that can offer suggestions. I'm in multiple Facebook groups, including a few wheelchair-specific ones, that have helped me to adapt my chair and improve both the safety of myself and my dogs, as well as our enjoyment.

Harris Dickenson, a dog trainer who specialises in training assistance dogs for people with rare disabilities

### Case Study: Mel

I suffer badly with my mental health, with anxiety and depression. Six years ago the thought of saying my name and running, let alone running for fun, would have been a huge joke to most people including myself. Without canicross I would never have had the courage to go out and run like I do now, especially in a big race environment! The sense of achievement and the confidence my dogs give me has allowed me to achieve more than I could possibly have imagined.

## Limitations for Canicross

While this book is based on how canicross can be a rewarding activity for dogs and is a particularly inclusive sport, because dogs and humans with various medical conditions can take part, this is provided that proper precautions and consultations with your vet and doctor are undertaken. The key to getting this right is to prioritise health, safety and well-being throughout your canicross journey. With guidance from your vet or doctor, and an understanding of your dog's specific needs, combined with your own, you can enjoy this sport together while promoting your physical fitness and mental health.

Canicross can be particularly beneficial for people who suffer with mental health conditions, and having your dog with you when running makes a difference to your motivation.

## The Importance of First Aid

When you have made the decision that you and your dog are both fit enough to take part in canicross, there is one last thing to consider in terms of health, and that is your first aid capabilities.

Canicross generally takes part in more remote locations, with fewer people around and less access to facilities for first aid. This means keeping your first aid training up to date, human and canine, is particularly important with a sport like canicross. Always ensure you keep a basic first aid kit handy, either on your person or in your car to allow you to deal with any problems quickly.

While injuries for your dog canicrossing are usually confined to paw injuries, small cuts or bruises and simple strains and sprains, if you are fully equipped to deal with them, you won't panic if anything does happen. It is more likely that you will experience injury before your dog, and so knowing your quickest route back to home or the car and being able to deal with the simple first aid issues you might encounter while canicrossing, will allow you to feel confident in what you are doing.

Keeping a first aid kit handy and your first aid training up to date is recommended if you're going to be canicrossing regularly.

## SUMMARY

- Make observations about your dog's vital signs to ensure you notice any changes.
- Monitor your dog's weight, skin, fur, paws and claws when you start canicrossing.
- Consider carefully your dog's age and any existing conditions they have before you start and consult with your vet if you have any concerns.
- Dogs with limiting conditions can take part in canicross with adaptions and specialist support.
- Humans with conditions can also enjoy the sport under guidance of a medical professional.
- Keep your first aid up to date, as you never know when you might need it.

If you have a dog who reacts to triggers in the environment, you may need to consider how you approach your training for canicross.

# CHAPTER 6
# Behavioural Considerations

The behavioural benefits of canicross have been discussed in detail earlier in this book, but as a society, we are seeing a rise in behavioural problems in our dogs. They can range from general anxiety to full-blown reactivity and cause problems when you are out and about and at home for your dog. For the purposes of this chapter, I will be using the term 'reactive' to refer to any anxious or unwanted behaviour your dog might display.

Canicross can give your dog an outlet for their excess energy in a safe way and help them to feel calmer, more relaxed and, in turn, improve their behaviour, but many people worry about taking their already anxious dog out canicrossing and wonder if they will encounter problems.

I get asked all the time if canicross is suitable for reactive dogs and the short answer is yes, canicross can be great for building a reactive dog's confidence. All the other dogs taking part should be on bungee leads, being kept under control, and space should be given for every dog. Canicross can give your dog socialisation with other dogs, people and environments in a controlled way, which can help them learn that these things are not scary.

This doesn't mean that canicross is suitable for all reactive dogs and careful consideration of your dog's specific behavioural needs is important to determine if this is going to be the sport for you.

Canicross can be good for reactive dogs to learn how to socialise safely in groups with other dogs who are under control and don't provide any threat.

## What Does Reactive Mean?

First, we need to define reactivity and what it means for your dog. Reactivity is the term frequently used to describe dogs that exhibit strong responses, often stemming from anxiety. The term becomes personal when you've shared your life with a reactive dog, as I have with three of my own.

Assuming that your reactive dog still has the capacity to be able to learn that a new, controlled situation can be fun for them, then canicross could be a game changer for them. However, reactivity is an extremely complex condition to deal with, and you will need to get very good at unpicking the cause of your dog's reactivity by identifying their triggers.

There are some dogs who may not only be reactive to other dogs, but also people. Some dogs will be reactive to moving vehicles, loud noises, changing light conditions and there is an almost endless list of things which could cause your dog to react to situations.

Without first identifying what the triggers are for your dog, you can't say for sure that your dog will enjoy canicross, because there may be too many triggers which your dog finds stressful, for them to get a positive experience. It is essential for your dog's well-being that you understand what is too much for them to cope with, and we look at that in terms of their 'threshold' for stress.

## Ladder of Aggression

Kendal Shepherd, a veterinarian and animal behaviourist, identified a ladder of aggression in dogs, and it correlates directly to the stress that they feel in certain situations. There are key behavioural signals you can look for in your dog to understand if they are beginning to move out of their comfort zone.

The ladder works from the bottom upwards in terms of a dog's response and their stress level, with 1 being acceptable and 11 being completely unacceptable. Where you determine that you will allow your dog to get to on the ladder is something that you should decide for yourself, but if your dog is displaying any of the signs from 4 on, you should be prepared that the behaviour could escalate quickly, and you don't want your dog to feel their only option is a physical reaction.

Not only will your dog lose trust in you if something negative happens in a canicross situation, but they will also learn to associate the things that led to the stress with being frightening and uncomfortable, so it is always better to stop any activity before it develops into this.

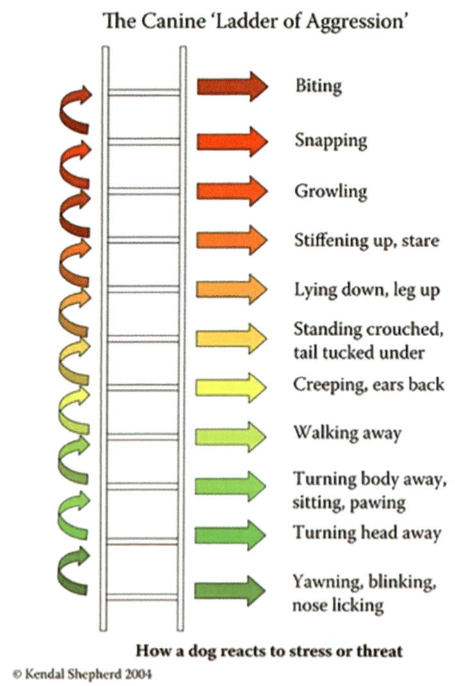


The canine 'Ladder of Aggression' gives us clear guidelines for levels of stress and anxiety in our dogs. Reproduced with permission from the *BSAVA Manual of Canine and Feline Behavioural Medicine*, 2nd edition. The canine 'Ladder of Aggression' concept was developed by Kendal Shepherd.

It is also worth remembering that there are laws in place to protect members of the public from dog attacks, and the UK Section 3 of the Dangerous Dogs Act 1991 covers dogs being 'dangerously out of control'. It is highly unlikely that being under control canicrossing, your dog would be considered dangerously out of control, but if they are stressed and lunging or snapping at other dogs and people, then you could fall under this legislation.

From a safety and ethical point of view for your dog, you should always aim to ensure your dog never ends up displaying behaviours at the higher end of the ladder of aggression.

## CANICROSS AND REACTIVE DOGS

Many reactive dogs love running with their owner. For dogs whose reactivity is caused by fear, the excitement they feel when canicrossing may override their anxiety of being around unfamiliar dogs and people. Canicross can provide a controlled environment for these dogs to socialise safely with other dogs and people, and help them build positive associations.

The sport is not suitable for all reactive dogs. Reactive behaviour can be caused by pain, frustration or fear. Advice should be sought from a qualified behaviourist before starting canicross, to ensure that reactive behaviour is not exacerbated by exposing the dog to stimuli that they cannot cope with.

Gemma Grisewood MSc, Clinical Animal Behaviourist and keen canicrosser

The best thing to do is to monitor what causes your dog to react and decide if the type of triggers are going to be a problem for your dog, once you have established that the behaviour isn't pain-related. You may see changes in your dog's behaviour, and so be aware of the things to look for if your dog isn't comfortable. You want your dog to enjoy canicross and to ensure it's always fun.

Canicross should always be a fun activity for both us and our dogs, and not stressful for either.

## Using Training to Help a Reactive Dog

We have covered the basic voice cues you should be teaching your dog for canicross, and with a reactive dog you can focus on some of these cues to help with your training.

*Straight on* encourages your dog to continue on the trail past any distractions and so with a reactive dog, your straight on cue can help your dog keep their forward focus if they are running alongside other dogs, or if another dog or trigger is in the vicinity of where you are running.

*Steady* is another good cue to focus on with a reactive dog, as getting them to slow down and think about the situation may give you the time to work out how to handle the trigger and get control so your dog gets the best experience when passing the problem.

*Back* or *behind* is crucial with a reactive dog, because if you can encourage your dog behind or in close with you, this can offer them the protection that you will provide. Being able to call your dog in close and offer them the reassurance that no harm will come to them will be extremely valuable in your training tool kit.

A back, behind, or in close cue for a reactive dog can really help to improve their confidence when passing things that might cause them anxiety.

## Other Trail Users and Their Dogs

When canicrossing, not everyone you meet will understand or appreciate what you are doing. I have had people comment, 'making a dog pull you is cruel' and canicrossers regularly hear 'that's cheating' when out running with our dogs. So, it is important to understand that, while it is obvious to you that loose dogs should be called away from a dog canicrossing, it is not always obvious to the dog walkers you might meet.

Your best 'weapon' against any annoying behaviour you might encounter is to be extremely polite, explain that your dog doesn't like to be approached and is working when they are in harness, a bit like a service dog.

Once you explain to someone that while canicross is fun, your dog is expected to do a job and not get distracted, most people will call their dogs away and make some space for you. It might be that you need to slow down and use your voice cues to call your dog in beside you, but anything you do to show that your dog is under control will highlight if their dog isn't, and usually results in your dog being left alone. You can also buy yellow anxious dog products which highlight your need for space.

What you do not want to do in these situations, is get frustrated with other trail users and end up creating tension or unease in your own dog. They will take their cues from you, and if you confidently negotiate any issues, it is more likely your dog will learn to trust you will handle the situation, and this takes away their need to react in a negative way.

Understand that whilst other canicrossers will understand your dog's need for space, the general pet-owning public may not; you can visually indicate this for them.

## Canicross Racing with a Reactive Dog

While canicross racing may be thrilling and a lot of fun, it can present unique challenges when your dog is reactive. Racing introduces an elevated level of excitement and nervousness, not only for you, but also for other competitors and their dogs. The competitive environment, combined with this adrenaline rush, makes it harder to control situations compared to casual canicross runs, even if you have already been running in group situations.

If your dog is reactive, you will want to consider whether canicross racing is suitable for you both. The heightened energy of a race and potential stress of other dogs being present can lead to situations where your dog is not comfortable and starts to move up the ladder of aggression as the triggers build in your dog's immediate environment. Always be cautious about your dog's comfort level in a racing scenario, because dogs feed off each other's energy, and a reactive dog in a competitive setting may face additional stress.

Carefully consider if canicross racing is going to be appropriate for your dog, as people and dogs become more competitive, and adrenalin can run higher at events.

## Racing Etiquette and Post-Race Dynamics

It is essential to remember the basics of trail etiquette during canicross races and to be sure you have control of your dog with your voice cues. Always make other trail users aware of your presence by calling out to them. Unfortunately, some participants may forget, or overlook these guidelines in a race situation, leading to an increased risk of incidents between dogs taking part and occasionally even runners. The competitive nature of some races can sometimes overshadow the human awareness of other dogs on the trail.

Post-race dynamics also play a crucial role in the management of your dog, whether they are reactive or not. Dogs may still be in a heightened state after the race due to the higher levels of adrenalin in their system, and owners might let their guard down. This can result in clashes between dogs, emphasising the importance of remaining vigilant of where your dog is and what behaviours they are displaying, even after the race finishes.

---

## A Checklist for Reactive Dog Running

Before beginning your canicross journey with a reactive dog, consider the following checklist:

***Vet approval***: ensure your dog is physically fit and has your vet's approval for a canicross training program.
***Proper equipment***: invest in the correct harness to suit your dog and a bungee lead to ensure your dog's comfort.
***Regular health checks***: have your dog regularly checked by a qualified therapist, such as a canine massage guild member, or veterinary physiotherapist to assess muscular health.
***Short, fun sessions***: keep initial sessions short, simple and enjoyable to leave your dog eager for more.
***Network of support***: establish a support network, including canicross coaches, behavioural experts and fellow runners, to guide you.

## SUMMARY

- Running with a reactive dog in a canicross setting requires careful consideration.
- With ongoing training, and a commitment to your dog's well-being you can still have a lot of fun.
- Understand your dog's triggers and make informed choices for them.
- Be aware of the triggers in different environments, and plan for them.
- Create positive and enjoyable experiences for both you and your dog by staying within your 'comfort zone'.
- Racing can be fun if you can manage your dog's reactivity to prevent incidents.

Nutrition for canicross dogs is a hot topic as many people are unsure how best to fuel their canine athlete for an increase in activity.

# CHAPTER 7
# Nutritional Considerations

Canicross is a sport that conjures up images of hard work and requires careful consideration of the nutritional needs of both the human athlete and their canine companion. Dogs are zoologically classified as carnivores because they have a short digestive tract designed for the quick breakdown of readily digestible material, but their digestive system is thought to be more adapted to an omnivorous diet. So, we need to make sure we are feeding them an appropriate diet based on many individual factors. Just as with human athletes, proper nutrition is crucial for the well-being, endurance and performance of canicross dogs. This chapter considers some of the key aspects of feeding your dog for optimal health when canicrossing.

## Timing

The time of day you feed your dog is important when canicrossing. Feeding shouldn't take place within an hour or two of any strenuous activity and, while it is generally thought to be more dangerous to feed your dog too close before a run, feeding a dog who has not cooled down sufficiently can also increase their chances of developing a condition called bloat.

Bloat is the day-to-day term for the veterinary condition known as Gastric dilatation-volvulus (GDV) which is potentially life-threatening if untreated. The dog's stomach becomes severely distended (bloated) with gas, fluid or food, and this puts pressure on the surrounding organs and decreases blood flow to and from these organs. In this bloating process, the stomach can become twisted, and this is more severe, as it obstructs blood supply to major organs and can impact blood flow throughout the whole body, resulting in shock.

Some dogs seem to be more prone to the condition and it is worth doing your research into whether your dog might suffer the condition more easily purely down to their breed. Deeper chested dogs and larger breeds seem to be more at risk, so bear this in mind when planning your canicross runs, factor in time for your dog to digest their food before running, and cool down properly after running to avoid any problems.

## Nutritional Requirements

Hydration is often overlooked when it comes to nutrition, and it is not only important for the absorption of a dog's food, including vitamins and minerals, but hydration is also essential for temperature regulation and overall well-being. Water is the first limiting nutrient, and any deficiency will impact performance faster than any dietary issues with other nutrients.

Adequate water intake is therefore crucial, and canicross dogs may need more water than usual due to increased activity and the potential for elevated temperatures during exercise. We have discussed how water on a canicross run is preferable to be able to hydrate your dog when running, but you also have to be aware of the problems associated with bloat if your dog drinks too much water when running; it is a careful balance.

Deep-chested dogs such as Hounds seem to be more predisposed to the condition of bloat, but all dogs should be fed with plenty of time either side of running.

### Baiting Water

You might hear people talking about 'baiting' their dog's water before they run. Simply put, this is adding something to your dog's water to encourage them to drink more and ensure they are fully hydrated before they run. It is a practice that has been used in sled dog racing for years to try to gain a competitive edge. However, unless you know exactly what your dog's optimum hydration intake will be for that run, based on the distance, the effort exerted, the temperature, and cooling processes needed as a result, then it would be quite difficult to get this correct by guessing. What you then risk is over-hydrating your dog, leading to them needing to rid themselves of the excess water more often, or in a worst-case scenario, bloat.

Other things you need to be aware of are water intoxication and the impact that too much water can have on the electrolyte balance in your dog's body. So, while it might sound like a good idea, if you are feeding your dog a decent, balanced diet and offering them free access to fresh water to hydrate themselves, there is probably no need to bait water for a canicross dog at all.

### Protein

The function of protein in a dog's diet is the same as in humans – to provide the building blocks for growth and repair of muscles, and to supply our dogs with a source of energy to support any activity they might be doing. Protein as a main source of energy for your dog, rather than fats or carbohydrate, isn't ideal due to the financial cost, metabolic cost and sustainability concerns.

Dogs will need protein in their diet to be able to meet their overall requirements. You will often see this used as an advertising tool for pet food manufacturers who state that their product is 'high in protein' to encourage owners to purchase them. However, you do need to be aware there are variable levels of quality in protein and not all protein has equal digestibility and nutritional value.

Carbohydrates, whilst considered by some as unnecessary in a canine diet, can help to maintain consistent performance in sports dogs.

The key to getting this right is to feed proteins from different sources, meat from different animals, but also from plants too and ensure that your dog has all the essential and non-essential amino acids derived from the protein in their food that they need.

It is obvious that our pet dogs will need a certain level of protein to maintain their muscles and provide them with the energy they need to function, but the canicross dog may require a higher protein intake compared to sedentary dogs to support their increased activity levels, and the potential increase in demand for repair and regeneration of body tissues because of the additional physical exercise.

## Lipids (Fats and Oils)

The function of fat in a dog's diet is to provide energy and many people will argue that it is the most important source of energy in our sports dogs, because it is thought to provide the most readily available and digestible energy for our canine athletes. Dogs use fat over carbohydrate, or protein, as an energy source and fat in the diet increases the energy density of a dog's food, which generally means you need to feed less volume of a higher-fat food to get the same energy output. Fat also provides fat-soluble vitamins and essential fatty acids needed for general health.

Essential fatty acids are important for dogs because they must be supplied by diet and regulate normal hormone function, circulation, immunity and inflammatory responses among other things. In terms of a canicross dog's diet, this is the one area where supplementation may be beneficial to ensure your dog is getting enough of the Omega-3 fatty acids, which support all aspects of the canicross including recovery.

In general, most complete, balanced dog foods will contain enough fat for the average pet dog, but if you are going to be significantly increasing the amount of exercise your dog is doing through canicross, then there may be some benefit in increasing the proportion of dietary fat in your dog's diet.

## Carbohydrates

The function of carbohydrate in a dog's diet is something often debated in the canine nutritional world, because there are some commentators who will argue that dogs don't need carbohydrate in their diet and cannot digest it. Indeed, there is no minimum dietary requirement for carbohydrate in the canine diet. Science has shown us, however, that carbohydrates can be useful in highly active dogs to aid performance and recovery.

To break down the use of carbohydrate in dogs it is necessary to understand the function of the elements of carbohydrate in fuelling dogs. Glucose is an essential simple carbohydrate, critical for all effective processes, and in sporting dogs who are working hard on consecutive days, this glucose stored in their muscles as glycogen can become depleted, and it can be problematic to refuel without overfeeding fat or protein.

Simple carbohydrates are easily digested by dogs, so if your dog is working hard, continuous days, the addition of carbohydrate in the diet can be beneficial for recovery and consistent performance.

## Vitamins and Minerals

Vitamins and minerals in a dog's diet play a crucial role in physiological processes and with a canine athlete, ensuring they have everything they need in their diet is essential to maintain optimal health. Most complete foods will have this balance of vitamins and minerals carefully designed to meet the needs of the pet dog. Working dog specific foods are available, but a label of 'working dog' on food might not mean it's been formulated for extra performance. It is worthwhile evaluating the ingredients of any dog food for nutrient composition and overall energy content if you are going to be doing a lot more exercise, and you feel your dog may need extra dietary support for this.

By evaluating your dog's diet and knowing their energy requirements, you can monitor their needs and feed them extra, or supplement their diet if required.

## Other Factors in Nutritional Requirements

Your dog will need different levels of all the main food groups at different life stages, and therefore taking into consideration your dog's age will help you to determine the most appropriate balance.

Bear in mind that different breeds or types of dogs may have differing requirements of nutrition. Some dogs have a genetic makeup which means that higher fat or higher protein is needed to support more rigorous exercise. Evaluating your dog for any breed-specific changes needed to their diet is advisable if you have any concerns.

Health conditions do not necessarily prevent your dog taking part in canicross, but they might influence nutritional needs for canicross, so looking at any changes necessary for your dog's individual health conditions with a qualified canine nutritionist would also be recommended.

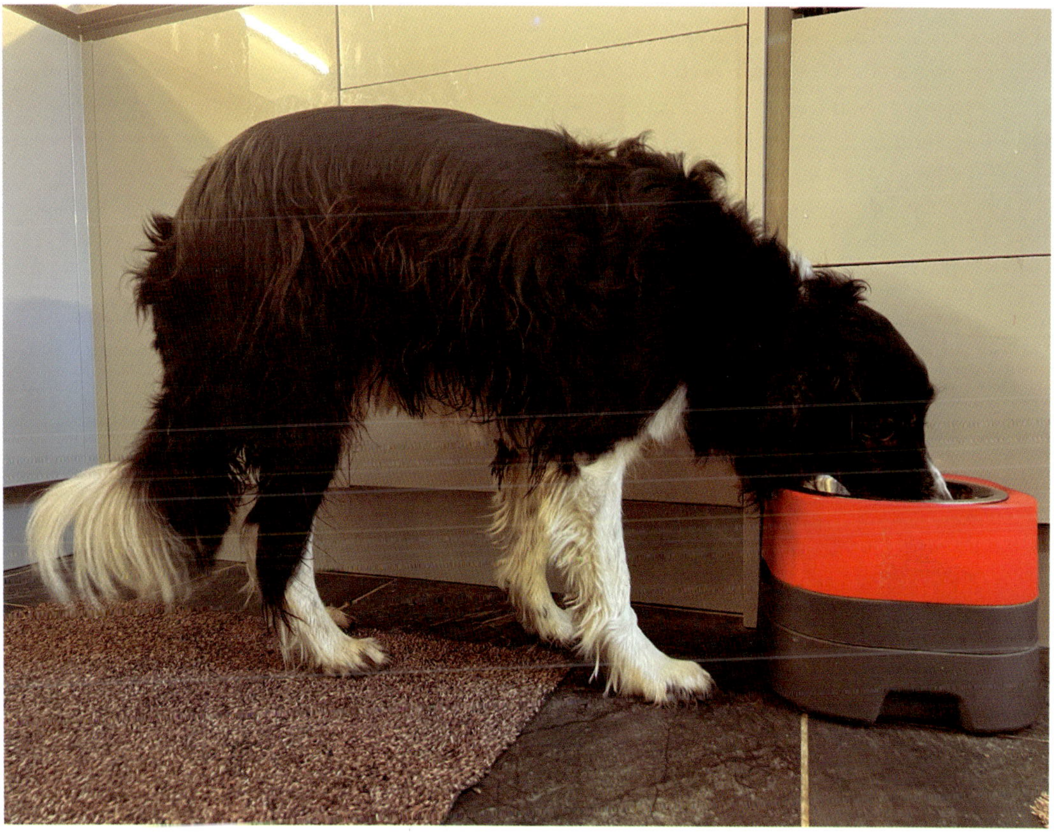

As your dog ages they may need different levels of the main food groups, so regularly review their diet to ensure it meets their current requirements.

## A Different Diet

Overall, your dog will probably be fine being fed their regular diet if you have selected a balanced and appropriate food that provides all the essential elements listed above. However, there are a few reasons why canicross dogs might need a different diet, which are considered below.

### Increased Energy Expenditure

Canicross dogs may have higher energy requirements due to the sustained and vigorous nature of their exercise. Canicross is described as an endurance sport in the dog world, even though our pet dogs are highly efficient runners and expend less effort running than we do. Diets should be adjusted to meet these increased energy demands if your dog shows any signs of fatigue or weight loss which can be attributed to the increased fuel requirements for activity.

### Muscle Maintenance

While canicross is considered a relatively low-impact sport on your dog's joints because they are highly efficient at running, they will still need flexible, strong and healthy muscles to cope with the pulling element. Being attached to a person, with the resistance of the extra weight, can create a strain on a dog's muscles, which you wouldn't have if your dog was free running. Therefore, adequate protein, essential for muscle repair and maintenance, should be provided for in the diet. This may need to be increased from the protein found in a standard complete diet for adult dogs to support your canicross dog's health and well-being.

The additional strain of pulling in harness may mean your dog needs a change in diet to support their muscles for the sport of canicross.

### Joint Health

Canicrossing involves running on various terrains, moving more than a sedentary pet dog while their joints are under load in the harness, and this may have a potential impact on joint health. Diets rich in Omega-3 fatty acids have been indicated as beneficial to help protect the joints in highly active dogs from wear and tear, so it might be worth considering supplementing your dog's diet with additional Omega-3. The best sources of this, for the bioavailability for your dog, is from marine-based products such as salmon oil, green-lipped mussels or marine algae. Whatever you decide to do in terms of supplementation, it is also worth checking that the products come from a reputable company using sustainable sources of Omega-3 that don't impact the environment.

### Hydration Needs

We know that increased activity levels necessitate proper hydration for ourselves and our dogs. Our dogs in particular need good levels of hydration for canicross, because they use an evaporative method of cooling themselves when warm through the heat generated by the activity. Wet or moist food, as well as ensuring access to fresh water, helps maintain hydration levels. If you feed kibble, you can increase your dog's water intake by adding some water to the bowl, to encourage them to drink more, but be careful not to add too much and upset the natural equilibrium of their diet.

## FEEDING YOUR DOG

Feeding the canicross dog is as much about how and when you will feed it as it is about what you feed. Our canicross dogs typically will have elevated requirements for dietary energy, protein and other micronutrients such as the antioxidant vitamin E. Timing of feeding around rest and activity is also critical to support digestion, nutrient assimilation and recovery.

As you increase the intensity, frequency and duration of any canicross endeavours, be alert to your dog's body condition, performance and recovery. This will allow you to make effective and proactive dietary choices.

Dr Jacqueline Boyd, Animal Scientist, Canine Consultant and Canicrosser

## SUMMARY

- Canicross dogs may not need additional volume to their food, but their diet may require some tweaks.
- Certain aspects of their diet such as fat, protein or even carbohydrate may need to be increased to provide optimal health.
- Always consult with a veterinarian and canine nutritionist to tailor a diet plan specific to your individual dog's needs.
- Consider factors such as age, breed, health conditions and activity levels when planning your dog's nutrition.
- Regular veterinary check-ups can ensure your canicross dog's nutritional needs are met.
- Adjustments can be made based on their evolving health and performance.

Once you have started your canicross journey, you may be keen to learn how to develop and get more involved with the sport.

# CHAPTER 8
# Future and Further Development

Now that you have more knowledge about how to get into canicross safely with your dog, and all the fun it can bring, you might want to start thinking about some longer-term goals and things you could do with your dog in the future. Canicross is a sport that is growing across the world, and so opportunities to progress your skills and knowledge are becoming more common.

## Canicross Groups

If you haven't already joined a canicross group, then you might be thinking about joining one. Being part of a local community of canicrossers is very rewarding and if you enjoy your new hobby, a canicross group is a great way to meet other people who share the same interest. Many canicross websites offer a list, or map, of groups so people can easily find their local group.

If you can't find a canicross group in your area, you might contemplate setting up your own canicross group. There are some things to consider with this, including making sure you have insurance covering you for third-party liability when running in a group. You can set up and advertise your group on social media for free without the need for a website or costly promotional materials. Local noticeboards can be a great way to gather interest, and local running clubs may be open to helping to set up a specific canicross element, although this is not usually covered under their regulations and liability insurance.

Canicross groups are a great way to expand your knowledge and experience canicrossing. If there isn't a local group, consider setting one up.

## Volunteering

Some of the more experienced canicrossers have gone on to offer assistance to their local rescue centres, taking out particularly high energy or difficult dogs, to give them something different to do outside of the kennel environment. This can be personally rewarding, and building good relationships with local rescue centres helps to share the benefits of canicross to a wider audience. Working with the local dog rescue community to promote responsible exercise for dogs who might be better kept on lead, particularly when they are first rehomed, can benefit everyone involved.

## Racing

Once you begin to get more confident with your voice cues and know your dog can cope with a group of canicross dogs, the next step is to go along and take part in a canicross race. There are human trail races allowing dogs, which may be more local to you, but bear in mind these races might not have specific canicross experienced organisers, and therefore not have the safety and welfare of the dogs as their priority. These events can be fun once you are more confident and capable as a canicrosser, but might be a bit daunting for a first race.

Race starts can be individual or mass starts, and both have advantages and disadvantages. With an individual start and a specific time, it can mean the start line is quieter, but also that you don't get so many people to observe on the start or finish. You may also get more overtaking if the times have been randomly allocated and not seeded (allocated by your estimated finish time).

Individual starts with a non-specific time can mean you've got more noise, but also that you have more people to watch, start and follow.

Mass starts are probably the most intimidating for people new to the sport, as everyone lines up together and all the excited dogs encourage each other into more excitement. It can mean you get a better run, as you know where your competitors are, and it can also mean less hanging about, as you all start off together. It is worth investigating the race start if any of this would be a concern, or would worry you with your dog.

Racing can be a lot of fun, but make sure you're prepared for being surrounded by a lot of excited dogs.

### Catering for Dogs on the Course

The canicross specific races will have taken into consideration the differences between a normal human trail run and a canicross trail run, sometimes by providing water on the course, but sometimes by something as simple as not expecting people to attend a race briefing with their dogs.

The noise of excited canicross dogs on a start line can be deafening, rendering any information being given as pointless, because you can't hear it. A canicross-specific race organiser will make sure you have all the information you need for your race prior to the start line, so keep this in mind when deciding which format will work best for you and your dog.

### Longer Distances

This will involve extra training time but can be very rewarding, particularly if you are not a speedy runner and prefer a slower pace of canicross. Races that cater for longer distance canicrossers tend to also be human trail races. The sport is still in its relative infancy, and therefore getting enough numbers for races to be viable means appealing to a wide range of runners. If you have raced shorter distances with your dog, and feel confident in being able to manage the needs of your dog on a longer run, then have a look at the canicross-friendly trail race organisers. It is also worth asking other races if they will allow you to run with your dog, as many will be open to this, if you take the responsibility for your dog and have your own insurance.

Longer-distance canicrossing can be built up to with your dog and might suit people or dogs who prefer a more leisurely pace of running.

### National Races

Canicross-specific race organisations exist to cater for canicrossers, some including the wheeled sports of bikejor (biking with your dog) and scootering with your dog. Organisations are being set up in countries all over the world to cater for a national championship race or race series.

Some championships are a prerequisite to filter athletes through for IFSS international races, and some provide a higher level of competition, or something to aim for, depending on the structure of the championship. You may need to attend a certain number of races in the championship to qualify for a place, as with regular running competitions.

### International Races

The IFSS (International Federation of Sleddog Sports) holds an international canicross championship race every year in a different country, and provided you have qualified through your own national governing body, you can take part.

There is another organisation called the International Canicross Federation (ICF), which also organises an annual championship and you don't need to qualify for this.

In addition, there are numerous races held in other countries which welcome canicrossers from abroad, and these can be great fun if you can afford them and navigate the various travel requirements for transporting dogs across country borders.

---

## Common Training Concerns

Injuries do happen in canicross, as in any sport, but if you have the right equipment, put in the time to train and ensure you are warming up, cooling down properly and not doing too much too soon, you will lower the risk of injury for both you and your dog.

***Tangled lines***: Lines can get tangled, especially in wooded areas or uneven terrain, but if you select a line of the correct length to give you the control you're looking for, then you should be better equipped to be able to avoid tripping if your dog does stop suddenly.

***Pulling***: Some dogs may pull more than others, making it difficult for the runner to maintain control of their dog, but you can alleviate this by getting the right equipment, putting in the time to train and building a bond with your dog, so they are working with you and not against you.

***Not pulling***: If you find your dog is not pulling you, you need to focus on getting the pull over short distances, and rewarding your dog for any forward movement into their harness. Build this up over time so you increase your distance, and always stop before your dog gets bored or distracted. Remember that canicross might not suit all dogs, and if you've had your dog checked for any physical problems, it may be that your dog just doesn't enjoy the sport, and you will have to accept a more leisurely style of running with your dog.

***Toileting***: You may not be able to stop your dog toileting completely during canicross sessions, and it's not fair to prevent them doing so if they need to, but you can help make toilet stops less frequent by encouraging them to go before you start your activity. You can use your voice cues and encourage them to continue forwards when running, rather than stop to mark the trail. If you choose when to stop, and regularly allow them the opportunity to toilet between sections of runs, they will learn what is 'work' time and what is 'toilet' time.

Not all dogs will naturally pull, and you can use your training to help, but not all dogs will want to pull you, so allow them to go at their own pace.

## SUMMARY

- Canicross is a developing and evolving sport.
- Rescue dogs can benefit from being introduced to canicross as an outlet for energy.
- Joining social groups or setting one up is a good way to progress.
- Races take part locally, nationally and internationally for those who want to be competitive.
- Longer distance canicross can be fun for those who prefer a steadier option.
- Many of the more common canicross concerns can be eliminated with patience and positive training.

Canicross has turned me into a fitter, healthier person and helped me to build a better bond with my dogs. I hope that in sharing what I've learnt, you and your dog can benefit from canicross too.

# APPENDIX
# Training Plans and Resources

This book has covered everything I wish I knew before I started canicrossing many years ago. I think if I had discovered canicross earlier with my previous dogs, I would have had more adventures with them and I would probably have been fitter and healthier much earlier on in my life.

My aim in writing this book is to encourage people to try the activity with their dog as part of building their bond, connecting owners with their highly active dogs, who may often be labelled 'difficult', and preventing the breakdown in communication that can happen when you both feel that you don't understand each other. I hope that by discussing the many factors involved in canicross and showing how accessible it is for most breeds and sizes of dogs, and most ages and levels of fitness in humans, that you will feel confident and well prepared to get going with your dog.

With the proper equipment, a commitment to training and consideration of any health implications, including any mental or physical conditions, you and your dog can enjoy canicross together. Now you have all the basic canicross information, and know how to get started, you might be keen to get harnessed up and out of the door. If your dog is old enough and you've considered all the other factors contained in this book, then there's nothing stopping you.

The following training plans are designed to be used at whichever stage you are currently at with your fitness, and they can be used progressively if you'd like to work through them.

All programmes include a RAMP warm-up routine that contains activities to *raise* the heart rate, *activate* and *mobilise* the muscles and *potentiate* the body for action.

## Pawsetter Level 1: An 8-Week, 3-Day Beginner Training Programme

Designed for unfit people and dogs,
to safely get to 5km (3mi) canicrossing together.

### Week 1

Warm-up should be 5–10 minutes.

**Exercises should include:**

*Raise:*

Both: slow walking to brisk walking – 2 minutes.

*Activate:*

Human: squats × 3.
Dog: sit to stand × 2.

*Mobilise:*

Human: calf raises × 3, hip circles × 2 in each direction.
Dog: wider to tighter circles × 2 in each direction.

*Potentiate:*

Both
Either point-to-point 'sprints', maximum of 2.
And/or (and better) line of 4 ground poles/sticks jog up and down maximum of 2 times.
Human: with high knees.
Dog: with precise paw lifts.

Use Week 1 to focus on your pull cues and your line out cues; incorporate this into your runs to set up your next run rep.

Run 1: run 1 minute, walk 2 minutes, repeat × 6.
Run 2: run 1 minute, walk 1 minute, repeat × 10.
Run 3: run 2 minutes, walk 2 minutes, repeat × 6.

Cool-down should be 5–10 minutes.

Both: brisk walking to slow walking – 2 minutes.

Dog: loose lead circles increasing in size × 2 in each direction.
Human: hip circles × 2 in each direction.

Dog: loose neck flexes × 2 in each direction aiming for the shoulder.
Human: upper body, quad and hamstring stretches, 2 × each limb.

Rest or cross train on the other days.

### Week 2

Warm-up should be 5–10 minutes.

**Exercises should include:**

*Raise:*

Both: slow walking to brisk walking – 2 minutes.

*Activate:*

Human: squats × 3.
Dog: sit to stand × 2, neck flexes × 2 in each direction aiming for the shoulder.

*Mobilise:*

Human: calf raises × 3, hip circles × 3 in each direction.
Dog: wider to tighter circles × 2 in each direction.

*Potentiate:*

Both

Either point-to-point 'sprints' maximum of 2.
And/or (and better) line of 4 ground poles/sticks jog up and down maximum of 2 times.
Human: with high knees.
Dog: with precise paw lifts.

Use week 2 to again focus on your pull cues and your line out cues, incorporate this into your runs to set up your next run rep.

Run 1: run 2 minutes, walk 2 minutes, repeat × 6.
Run 2: run 3 minutes, walk 3 minutes, repeat × 5.
Run 3: run 3 minutes, walk 2 minutes, repeat × 6.

Cool-down should be 5–10 minutes.

Both: brisk walking to slow walking – 2 minutes.

Dog: loose lead circles increasing in size × 3 in each direction.
Human: hip circles × 2 in each direction.

Dog: loose neck flexes × 2 in each direction aiming for the shoulder.
Human: upper body, quad and hamstring stretches, 2 × each limb.

Rest or cross train on the other days.

## Week 3

Warm-up should be 5–10 minutes.

**Exercises should include:**

*Raise:*
Both: slow walking to brisk walking – 2 minutes.

*Activate:*
Human: squats × 5.
Dog: sit to stand × 3, neck flexes × 3 in each direction aiming for the shoulder.

*Mobilise:*
Human: calf raises × 5, hip circles × 3 in each direction.
Dog: wider to tighter circles × 3 in each direction.

*Potentiate:*
Both
Either point-to-point 'sprints' maximum of 3.
And/or (and better) line of 4 ground poles/sticks jog up and down maximum of 3 times.
Human: with high knees.
Dog: with precise paw lifts.

Use Week 3 to again focus on your pull cues and your line out cues, incorporate this into your runs to set up your next run rep but also start to add in directional cue training when you can, start training this in your walk sets.

Run 1: run 3 minutes, walk 2 minutes, repeat × 6.
Run 2: run 4 minutes, walk 2 minutes, repeat × 5.
Run 3: run 5 minutes, walk 3 minutes, repeat × 4.

Cool-down should be 5–10 minutes.

Both: brisk walking to slow walking – 2 minutes.

Dog: loose lead circles increasing in size × 3 in each direction.
Human: hip circles × 3 in each direction.

Dog: loose neck flexes × 2 in each direction aiming for the shoulder.
Human: upper body, quad and hamstring stretches 3 × each limb.

Rest or cross train on the other days.

## Week 4

Warm-up should be 5–10 minutes.

**Exercises should include:**

*Raise:*

Both: slow walking to brisk walking – 3 minutes.

*Activate:*

Human: squats × 5.

Dog: sit to stand × 3, neck flexes × 3 in each direction aiming for the shoulder.

*Mobilise:*

Human: calf raises × 5, hip circles × 3 in each direction.

Dog: wider to tighter circles × 3 in each direction.

*Potentiate:*

Both

Either point-to-point 'sprints' maximum of 4.

And/or (and better) line of 4 ground poles/sticks jog up and down maximum of 3 times.

Human: with high knees.

Dog: with precise paw lifts.

Week 4: continue your focus on your pull cues, your line out cues, and your directional cue training and start to add in a steady cue to set you up for your walk sets.

Run 1: run 5 minutes, walk 3 minutes, repeat × 4.

Run 2: run 6 minutes, walk 2 minutes, repeat × 4.

Run 3: run 6 minutes, walk 2 minutes, repeat × 4.

Cool-down should be 5–10 minutes.

Both: brisk walking to slow walking – 3 minutes.

Dog: loose lead circles increasing in size × 3 in each direction.

Human: hip circles × 3 in each direction.

Dog: loose neck flexes, 3 in each direction aiming for the shoulder.

Human: upper body, quad and hamstring stretches 3 × each limb.

Rest or cross train on the other days.

## Week 5

Warm-up should be approximately 10 minutes.

**Exercises should include:**

*Raise:*

Both: slow walking to brisk walking – 3 minutes.

*Activate:*

Human: squats × 5.

Dog: sit to stand × 3, neck flexes × 3 in each direction aiming for the ribs.

*Mobilise:*

Human: calf raises × 5, hip circles × 3 in each direction.

Dog: wider to tighter circles × 3 in each direction.

*Potentiate:*

Both

Either point-to-point 'sprints', maximum of 4.

And/or (and better) line of 6 ground poles/sticks jog up and down maximum of 4 times.

Human: with high knees.

Dog: with precise paw lifts.

Week 5: continue your focus on your pull cues, your line out cues, your directional cue training and your steady cue.

Run 1: run 7 minutes, walk 3 minutes, repeat × 3.
Run 2: run 7 minutes, walk 3 minutes, repeat × 3, run 5 minutes.
Run 3: run 8 minutes, walk 2 minutes, repeat × 3, run 5 minutes.

Cool-down should be approximately 10 minutes.

Both: brisk walking to slow walking – 3 minutes.
Dog: loose lead circles increasing in size × 3 in each direction.
Human: hip circles × 3 in each direction.

Dog: loose neck flexes, 3 in each direction aiming for the ribs.
Human: upper body, quad and hamstring stretches 4 × each limb.

Rest or cross train on the other days.

## Week 6

Warm-up should be approximately 10 minutes.

**Exercises should include:**

***Raise:***
Both: slow walking to brisk walking – 3 minutes.

***Activate:***
Human: squats × 8.
Dog: sit to stand × 5, neck flexes × 3 in each direction aiming for the ribs.

***Mobilise:***
Human: calf raises × 8, hip circles × 3 in each direction.
Dog: wider to tighter circles × 4 in each direction.

***Potentiate:***
Both
Either point to-point 'sprints' maximum of 4.
And/or (and better) line of 4 ground poles/sticks jog up and down maximum of 4 times.
Human: with high knees.
Dog: with precise paw lifts.

Week 6: continue your focus on your pull cues, your line out cues, your directional cue training, your steady cue and now have a look at training a straight on cue.

Run 1: run 8 minutes, walk 2 minutes, repeat × 3, run 5 minutes.
Run 2: run 9 minutes, walk 2 minutes, repeat × 2, run 5 minutes.
Run 3: run 9 minutes, walk 1 min, repeat × 3, run 5 minutes.
Cool-down should be approximately 10 minutes.

Both: brisk walking to slow walking – 3 minutes.
Dog: loose lead circles increasing in size × 3 in each direction.
Human: hip circles × 5 in each direction.

Dog: loose neck flexes, 3 in each direction aiming for the ribs.
Human: upper body, quad and hamstring stretches 5 × each limb.

Rest or cross train on the other days.

## Week 7

Warm-up should be approximately 10 minutes.

**Exercises should include:**

***Raise:***

Both: slow walking to brisk walking – 3 minutes.

***Activate:***

Human: squats × 10.

Dog: sit to stand × 5, neck flexes × 3 in each direction aiming for the hips.

***Mobilise:***

Human: calf raises × 10, hip circles × 3 in each direction.

Dog: wider to tighter circles × 5 in each direction.

***Potentiate:***

Both

Either point-to-point 'sprints' maximum of 6.

And/or (and better) line of 6 ground poles/sticks jog up and down maximum of 4 times.

Human: with high knees.

Dog: with precise paw lifts.

Week 7: you should have developed a reliable pull cue, a line out cue, your directional cues should be getting better, your steady cue and straight on cue should be progressing and you can now look at training a behind cue.

Run 1: run 10 minutes, walk 2 minutes, repeat × 3.

Run 2: run 10 minutes, walk 2 minutes, repeat × 3.

Run 3: run 12 minutes, walk 2 minutes, repeat × 2, run 8 minutes.

Cool-down should be approximately 10 minutes.

Both: brisk walking to slow walking – 3 minutes.

Dog: loose lead circles increasing in size × 3 in each direction.

Human: hip circles × 5 in each direction.

Dog: loose neck flexes, 3 in each direction aiming for the hips.

Human: upper body, quad and hamstring stretches 5 × each limb.

Rest or cross train on the other days.

## Week 8

Warm-up should be 10 minutes.

**Exercises should include:**

***Raise:***

Both: slow walking to brisk walking – 3 minutes.

***Activate:***

Human: squats × 10.

Dog: sit to stand × 5, neck flexes × 3 in each direction aiming for the hips.

***Mobilise:***

Human: calf raises × 10, hip circles × 3 in each direction.

Dog: wider to tighter circles × 5 in each direction.

***Potentiate:***

Both

Either point-to-point 'sprints' maximum of 6.

And/or (and better) line of 6 ground poles/sticks jog up and down maximum of 4 times.

Human: with high knees.

Dog: with precise paw lifts.

Week 8: you should have developed a reliable pull cue, a line out cue, your directional cues should be getting better, your steady cue and straight on cue should be progressing, and you should now be training a reliable behind cue.

Run 1: run 15 minutes, walk 2 minutes, repeat × 2.

Run 2: run 12 minutes, walk 1 min, repeat × 3.

Run 3: complete your 5km (3mi) with no walking.

Cool-down should be approximately 10 minutes.

Both: brisk walking to slow walking – 3 minutes.

Dog: loose lead circles increasing in size × 3 in each direction.

Human: hip circles × 5 in each direction.

Dog: loose neck flexes, 3 in each direction aiming for the hips.

Human: upper body, quad and hamstring stretches 5 × each limb.

Rest or cross train on the other days.

## Pawsetter Level 2: A 6-Week, 3-Day Beginner Canicross Training Programme

Designed for people and dogs with a base level of fitness, to comfortably get to 5km (3mi) canicrossing together.

### Week 1

Warm-up should be 5–10 minutes.

**Exercises should include:**

***Raise:***

Both: slow walking to brisk walking – 2 minutes.

***Activate:***

Human: squats × 5.

Dog: sit to stand × 3.

***Mobilise:***

Human: calf raises × 5, hip circles × 3 in each direction.

Dog: wider to tighter circles × 3 in each direction.

***Potentiate:***

Both

Either point-to-point 'sprints' maximum of 4.

And/or (and better) line of 4 ground poles/sticks jog up and down maximum of 2 times.

Human: with high knees.

Dog: with precise paw lifts.

Week 1: use week 1 to focus on your pull cues and your line out cues, incorporate this into your runs to set up your next run rep.

Run 1: run 1 minute, walk 1 min, repeat × 10.

Run 2: run 2 minutes, walk 4 minutes, repeat × 5.

Run 3: run 2 minutes, walk 4 minutes, repeat × 5.

Cool-down should be 5–10 minutes.

Both: brisk walking to slow walking – 2 minutes.

Dog: loose lead circles increasing in size × 3 in each direction.

Human: hip circles × 3 in each direction.

Dog: loose neck × 2 in each direction aiming for the shoulder.

Human: upper body, quad and hamstring stretches 3 × each limb.

Rest or cross train on the other days.

### Week 2

Warm-up should be 5–10 minutes.

**Exercises should include:**

***Raise:***

Both: slow walking to brisk walking – 2 minutes.

***Activate:***

Human: squats × 5.

Dog: sit to stand × 3, neck flexes × 2 in each direction aiming for the shoulder.

***Mobilise:***

Human: calf raises × 5, hip circles × 3 in each direction.

Dog: wider to tighter circles × 3 in each direction.

***Potentiate:***

Both

Either point-to-point 'sprints' maximum of 4.
And/or (and better) line of 4 ground poles/sticks jog up and down maximum of 2 times.
Human: with high knees.
Dog: with precise paw lifts.

Week 2: use week 2 to again focus on your pull cues and your line out cues, incorporate this into your runs to set up your next run rep, but also start to add in directional cue training when you can, start training this in your walk sets.

Run 1: run 3 minutes, walk 3 minutes, repeat × 4.
Run 2: run 3 minutes, walk 3 minutes, repeat × 4.
Run 3: run 5 minutes, walk 3 minutes, repeat × 3.

Cool-down should be 5–10 minutes.

Both: brisk walking to slow walking – 2 minutes.

Dog: loose lead circles increasing in size × 3 in each direction.
Human: hip circles × 3 in each direction.

Dog: loose neck flexes, × 2 in each direction aiming for the shoulder.
Human: upper body, quad and hamstring stretches 3 × each limb.

Rest or cross train on the other days.

## Week 3

Warm-up should be 5–10 minutes.

**Exercises should include:**
*Raise:*
Both: slow walking to brisk walking – 3 minutes.

*Activate:*
Human: squats × 8.
Dog: sit to stand × 5, neck flexes × 3 in each direction aiming for the shoulder.

*Mobilise:*
Human: calf raises × 8, hip circles × 3 in each direction.
Dog: wider to tighter circles × 3 in each direction.

*Potentiate:*
Both
Either point-to-point 'sprints' maximum of 6.
And/or (and better) line of 6 ground poles/sticks jog up and down maximum of 2 times.
Human: with high knees.
Dog: with precise paw lifts.

Week 3: continue your focus on your pull cues, your line out cues, and your directional cue training and start to add in a steady cue to set you up for your walk sets.

Run 1: run 7 minutes, walk 2 minutes, repeat × 3.
Run 2: run 8 minutes, walk 2 minutes, repeat × 3.
Run 3: run 8 minutes, walk 2 minutes, repeat × 3.

Cool-down should be 5–10 minutes.

Both: brisk walking to slow walking – 3 minutes.

Dog: loose lead circles increasing in size × 3 in each direction.
Human: hip circles × 5 in each direction.

Dog: loose neck flexes, 3 in each direction aiming for the shoulder.
Human: upper body, quad and hamstring stretches 5 × each limb.

Rest or cross train on the other days.

## Week 4

Warm-up should be approximately 10 minutes.

**Exercises should include:**

***Raise:***
Both: slow walking to brisk walking – 3 minutes.

***Activate:***
Human: squats × 8.
Dog: sit to stand × 5, neck flexes × 3 in each direction aiming for the ribs.

***Mobilise:***
Human: calf raises × 8, hip circles × 3 in each direction.
Dog: wider to tighter circles × 3 in each direction.

***Potentiate:***
Both
Either point-to-point 'sprints' maximum of 6.
And/or (and better) line of 6 ground poles/sticks jog up and down maximum of 2 times.
Human: with high knees.
Dog: with precise paw lifts.

Week 4: continue your focus on your pull cues, your line out cues, your directional cue training and your steady cue.

Run 1: run 8 minutes, walk 2 minutes, repeat × 3.
Run 2: run 10 minutes, walk 2 minutes, repeat × 2, run 5 minutes.
Run 3: run 8 minutes, walk 2 minutes, repeat × 3.

Cool-down should be approximately 10 minutes.

Both: brisk walking to slow walking – 3 minutes.

Dog: loose lead circles increasing in size × 3 in each direction.
Human: hip circles × 5 in each direction.

Dog: loose neck flexes, 3 in each direction aiming for the ribs.
Human: upper body, quad and hamstring stretches 5 × each limb.

Rest or cross train on the other days.

## Week 5

Warm-up should be approximately 10 minutes.

**Exercises should include:**

***Raise:***
Both: slow walking to brisk walking – 3 minutes.

***Activate:***
Human: squats × 10.
Dog: sit to stand × 5, neck flexes × 3 in each direction aiming for the ribs.

***Mobilise:***
Human: calf raises × 10, hip circles × 3 in each direction.
Dog: wider to tighter circles × 5 in each direction.

***Potentiate:***
Both
Either point-to-point 'sprints' maximum of 6.
And/or (and better) line of 6 ground poles/sticks jog up and down maximum of 4 times.
Human: with high knees.
Dog: with precise paw lifts.

Week 5: continue your focus on your pull cues, your line out cues, your directional cue training,

your steady cue and now have a look at training a straight on cue.

Run 1: run 9 minutes, walk 1 minute, repeat × 3.
Run 2: run 11 minutes, walk 2 minutes, repeat × 2, run 5 minutes.
Run 3: run 8 minutes, walk 2 minutes, repeat × 3.

Cool-down should be approximately 10 minutes.

Both: brisk walking to slow walking – 3 minutes.

Dog: loose lead circles increasing in size × 3 in each direction.
Human: hip circles × 5 in each direction.

Dog: loose neck flexes, 3 in each direction aiming for the ribs.
Human: upper body, quad and hamstring stretches 5 × each limb.

Rest or cross train on the other days.

## Week 6

Warm-up should be 5–10 minutes.

**Exercises should include:**
*Raise:*
Both: slow walking to brisk walking – 3 minutes.

*Activate:*
Human: squats × 10.
Dog: sit to stand × 5, neck flexes × 3 in each direction aiming for the hips.

*Mobilise:*
Human: calf raises × 10, hip circles × 3 in each direction.
Dog: wider to tighter circles × 5 in each direction.

*Potentiate:*
Both
Either point-to-point 'sprints' maximum of 6.
And/or (and better) line of 6 ground poles/sticks jog up and down maximum of 4 times.
Human: with high knees.
Dog: with precise paw lifts.

Week 6: you should have developed a reliable pull cue, a line out cue, your directional cues should be getting better, your steady cue and straight on cue should be progressing and you can now look at training a behind cue.

Run 1: run 15 minutes, walk 1 minute, repeat × 2.
Run 2: run 8 minutes, walk 2 minutes, repeat × 3.
Run 3: complete your 5km (3mi).

Cool-down should be approximately 10 minutes.

Both: brisk walking to slow walking – 3 minutes.

Dog: loose lead circles increasing in size × 3 in each direction.
Human: hip circles × 5 in each direction.

Dog: loose neck flexes, 3 in each direction aiming for the hips.
Human: upper body, quad and hamstring stretches 5 × each limb.

Rest or cross train on the other days.

## Pawsetter Level 3: A 6-Week, 3-Day Intermediate Canicross Training Programme

Designed for people and dogs with a good level of fitness who have already been running together, but perhaps not canicrossing together, to get to a 5km (3mi) canicross race together.

Your warm-up for every run:
Warm-up should be 10 minutes.

**Exercises should include:**

*Raise:*
Both: slow walking to brisk walking – 2 minutes.

*Activate:*
Human: squats × 10.
Dog: sit to stand × 5.

*Mobilise:*
Human: calf raises × 10, hip circles × 5 in each direction, arm circles × 5 in each direction.
Dog: wider to tighter circles × 3 in each direction.

*Potentiate:*
Both
Either point-to-point 'sprints' maximum of 6.
And/or (and better) line of up to 6 ground poles/sticks jog up and down a maximum of 6 reps.
Human: with high knees.
Dog: with precise paw lifts.

Your cool-down for every run:
Cool-down should be 5–10 minutes.

Both: brisk walking to slow walking – 3 minutes.

Dog: loose lead circles increasing in size × 3 in each direction.
Human: hip circles × 5 in each direction.

Dog: loose neck flexes, × 3 in each direction aiming for the shoulder.
Human: upper body, quad and hamstring stretches 5 × each limb.

### Week 1

Warm-up and cool-down.

Week 1: use week 1 to focus on your pull cues and your line out cues, and incorporate this into your runs to set up your next run from a walk.

Run 1: run/walk 15–20 minutes of a 30–40 minute walk.
Run 2: run/walk 20–25 minutes of a 30–40 minute walk.
Run 3: 10-minute easy run, 4 × 1 minute sprints with 2 minutes' rest, 10-minute easy run.
Run 4: 30-minute easy run.

Rest or cross train on the other days.

## Week 2

Week 2: use week 2 to again focus on your pull cues and your line out cues, incorporate this into your runs to set up your next run rep from walk, but also start to add in directional cue training when you can; start training this in your walk sets.

Warm-up and cool-down.

Run 1: run/walk 20 minutes of a 30–40 minute walk.
Run 2: run/walk 25 minutes of a 30–40 minute walk.
Run 3: 10-minute easy run, 5 × 2 minute sprints with 2 minutes' rest, 10-minute easy run.
Run 4: 35-minute easy run.

Rest or cross train on the other days.

## Week 3

Week 3: continue your focus on your pull cues, your line out cues, and your directional cue training, and start to add in a steady cue to set you up for your walk sets.

Warm-up and cool-down.

Run 1: run/jog 20 minutes of a 30–40 minute walk.
Run 2: run/jog 25 minutes of a 30–40 minute walk.
Run 3: 10-minute easy run, 6 × 2 minute sprints with 2 minutes' rest, 10-minute easy run.
Run 4: 40-minute easy run.

Rest or cross train on the other days.

## Week 4

Week 4: continue your focus on your pull cues, your line out cues, your directional cue training and your steady cue.

Warm-up and cool-down.

Run 1: 10-minute easy run, 10-minute tempo run (race pace), 10-minute easy run.
Run 2: run/jog 25 minutes of a 30–40 minute walk.
Run 3: 10-minute easy run, 8 × 2 minute sprints with 1 minute's rest, 10-minute easy run.
Run 4: 45-minute easy run.

Rest or cross train on the other days.

### Week 5

Week 5: continue your focus on your pull cues, your line out cues, your directional cue training, your steady cue and now have a look at training a straight on cue.

Warm-up and cool-down.

Run 1: 10-minute easy run, 10-minute tempo run (race pace), 10-minute easy run.
Run 2: run 25 minutes of a 30–40 minute walk.
Run 3: 10-minute easy run, 3 × 3 minute sprints with 2 minutes' rest, 10-minute easy run.
Run 4: 35-minute easy run.

Rest or cross train on the other days.

### Week 6

Week 6: you should have developed a reliable pull cue, a line out cue, your directional cues should be getting better, your steady cue and straight on cue should be progressing and you can now look at training a behind cue.

Warm-up and cool-down.

Run 1: 10-minute easy run, 3 × 2 minute sprints with 2 minutes' rest, 10 minute easy run.
Run 2: run 25 minutes of a 30–40 minute walk.
Run 3: rest/cross train or easy 15-minute run.
Run 4: complete your 5km (3mi) race together.

Rest or cross train on the other days.

## Pawsetter Level 4: A 6-Week, 3-Day Intermediate 10km (6mi) Canicross Training Programme

Designed for people and dogs with a good level of fitness, who have already been canicrossing together to a 5km (3mi) distance, to get to a steady 10km (6mi) canicross run or race together.

Your warm-up for every run:
Warm-up should be 10–15 minutes.

**Exercises should include:**

*Raise:*
Both: slow walking to brisk walking – 3–4 minutes.

*Activate:*
Human: squats × 10.
Dog: sit to stand × 5.

*Mobilise:*
Human: calf raises × 10, lunges × 5 on each side, hip circles × 5 in each direction, arm circles × 5 in each direction.
Dog: wider to tighter circles × 3 in each direction, stand to down × 5, neck flexes × 3 aiming for the shoulder.

*Potentiate:*
Both
Either point-to-point 'sprints' maximum of 6.
And/or (and better) line of up to 6 ground poles/sticks jog up and down a maximum of 6 reps.
Human: with high knees.
Dog: with precise paw lifts.

Your cool-down for every run:
Cool-down should be 10 minutes.

Both: brisk walking to slow walking – 3–4 minutes.

Dog: loose lead circles increasing in size × 3 in each direction.
Human: hip circles × 5 in each direction, arm circles × 5.

Dog: loose neck flexes, × 3 in each direction aiming for the hip.
Human: upper body, quad and hamstring stretches 5 × each limb.

Don't forget to train your canicross voice cues on every run.

### Week 1

Run 1: 3-mile easy run.
Run 2: 2.5-mile run, incorporating 3 × 100 metre speed sets.
Run 3: 3-mile run, incorporating hill work/uneven terrain.

### Week 2

Run 1: 3-mile easy run.
Run 2: 2.5-mile run, incorporating 3 × 150 metre speed sets.
Run 3: 3.5-mile run, incorporating hill work/uneven terrain.

### Week 3

Run 1: 3-mile easy run.
Run 2: 3-mile run, incorporating 3 × 200 metre speed sets.
Run 3: 4-mile run, incorporating hill work/uneven terrain.

### Week 4

Run 1: 3-mile easy run.
Run 2: 3.5-mile run, incorporating 5 × 200 metre speed sets.
Run 3: 5-mile run, incorporating hill work/uneven terrain.

### Week 5

Run 1: 4-mile easy run.
Run 2: 3.5-mile run, incorporating 5 × 200 metre speed sets.
Run 3: 5-mile run, incorporating hill work/uneven terrain.

### Week 6

Run 1: 4-mile easy run.
Run 2: 3.5-mile run incorporating 5 × 200 metre speed sets.
Run 3: 10km (6mi) day – remember to warm up and cool down properly and enjoy it!

## Pawsetter Level 5: A 6-Week, 3-Day Advanced 10km (6mi) Canicross Training Programme

Designed for people and dogs with a good level of fitness who have already been canicrossing together to a 10km distance, to get faster and stronger.

Your warm-up for every run:
Warm-up should be 10–15 minutes.

**Exercises should include:**

*Raise:*
Both: slow walking to brisk walking – 3–4 minutes.

*Activate:*
Human: squats × 10.
Dog: sit to stand × 5.

*Mobilise:*
Human: calf raises × 10, lunges × 5 on each side, hip circles × 5 in each direction, arm circles × 5 in each direction.
Dog: wider to tighter circles × 3 in each direction, stand to down × 5, neck flexes × 3 aiming for the shoulder.

*Potentiate:*
Both
Either point-to-point 'sprints' maximum of 6.
And/or (and better) line of up to 6 ground poles/sticks jog up and down a maximum of 6 reps.
Human: with high knees.
Dog: with precise paw lifts.

Your cool-down for every run:
Cool-down should be 10 minutes.

Both: brisk walking to slow walking – 3–4 minutes.

Dog: loose lead circles increasing in size × 3 in each direction.
Human: Hip circles × 5 in each direction, arm circles × 5.

Dog: loose neck flexes, × 3 in each direction aiming for the hip.
Human: upper body, quad and hamstring stretches 5 × each limb.

Don't forget to train your canicross voice cues on every run.

### Week 1

Run 1: 20-minute easy run, 3 × 100 metre sprints, 12 × 30 seconds on, 30 seconds off, at top speed, 10-minute easy run, cool down.
Run 2: 1-hour easy run, on easy terrain.
Run 3: 20-minute easy run, 3 × 100 metre sprints, 3 × 1km at race pace with 3-minute recovery, 10-minute easy run, cool down.

### Week 2

Run 1: 20-minute easy run, 3 × 100 metre sprints, 10 × 45 seconds on, 45 seconds off, at top speed, 10-minute easy run, cool down.
Run 2: 1 hour 10-minute easy run, on easy terrain.
Run 3: 20-minute easy run, 3 × 100 metre sprints, 4 × 1km at race pace with 3-minute recovery, 10-minute easy run, cool down.

### Week 3

Run 1: 20-minute easy run, 3 × 100 metre sprints, 10 × 1 minute on, 1 minute off, at top speed, 10-minute easy run, cool down.
Run 2: 1 hour 15-minute easy run, on easy terrain.
Run 3: 20-minute easy run, 3 × 100 metre sprints, 2 × 2km at race pace with 4-minute recovery, 10-minute easy run, cool down.

### Week 4

Run 1: 20-minute easy run, 3 × 100 metre sprints, 8 × 1 minute 30 seconds on, 1 minute off, at top speed, 10-minute easy run, cool down.
Run 2: 1 hour 15-minute easy run, on easy terrain.
Run 3: 20-minute easy run, 3 × 100 metre sprints, 2km at race pace with 4-minute recovery, 1km at race pace with 4-minute recovery, 2km at race pace with 4-minute recovery, 10-minute easy run, cool down.

### Week 5

Run 1: 20-minute easy run, 3 × 100 metre sprints, 15 × 30 seconds on, 30 seconds off, at top speed, 10-minute easy run, cool down.
Run 2: 1 hour 20-minute easy run, on easy terrain.
Run 3: 20-minute easy run, 3 × 100 metre sprints, 4 × 1km at race pace with 3-minute recovery, 10-minute easy run, cool down.

### Week 6

Run 1: 20-minute easy run, 3 × 100 metre sprints, 2 × 1km at race pace with 2-minute recovery, 10-minute easy run, cool down.
Run 2: 30-minute easy run, on easy terrain.
Run 3: Race day – remember to warm up and cool down properly and run your fastest 10km (6mi)!

### Rest Days

The incorporation of rest days and cross training into your training plan is very important for the overall health and well-being of you and your dog. Ensure you use your rest/cross train days to do activities for you which contribute to your strength, flexibility, balance and proprioception and have at least one full day off a week.

**Some suitable activities are:**

- Walking
- Biking
- Swimming
- Pilates
- Yoga
- Weight training
- Gym classes

For your dog you need to make sure you incorporate activities that contribute to their strength, flexibility, balance and proprioception, but also which allow them the opportunity to exhibit other natural behaviours and make sure they have at least one full day off a week.

**Some suitable activities are:**

- Walking
- Swimming
- Mantrailing
- Scentwork
- Canine conditioning
- Dog training classes

## Canicross Voice Cues

Train your canicross voice cues on every run and, where not specified in the plan, using the general guidelines below will help you develop your skills with your dog:

- Line out and pull cues: practise these for your speed sessions, encouraging your dog on every set to line out and pull in front for every burst of speed.
- Steady cue: use this to slow down for every recovery set in the plan.
- Direction cues: practise these on the easier sections of the plan if you can, so you don't have to think about too many things at once.
- Over cue: develop this around natural obstacles on the easier sections of your run; only train this when your directions are solid on sections of trail with no turns.
- Straight on cue: practise this in your sprint sessions to encourage your dog past any distractions.
- Back or behind cue: this is your cue for your dog to get beside or behind you, and you should be practising this on any downhill or tricky sections of trail, so your dog starts to automatically realise that downhill means a slowdown in speed and to come in close to you.

# Further Information

## Books

### Movement and Gait

Fischer, Professor Dr, *Dogs in Motion* (VDH Service GmbH, 2011)
Gillette, Robert L., *Athletic and Working Dog: Functional Anatomy and Biomechanics* (2019)
Elliott, Rachel Page, *Dogsteps: A New Look* (Companion House Books, 3rd edition, 2014)

### Canine Athlete Health

Davies, Lowri, *Care of the Canine Athlete* (The Pet Book Publishing Company Ltd, 2018)
Fretwell, E., Lawrence-Baker, R., *et al*, *Dogs in Detail* (2022)
Case, Linda P., *The Dog: Its Behavior, Nutrition, and Health* (Wiley-Blackwell, 2nd edition, 2005)

### Canine First Aid

http://www.rachelbean.co.uk

### Behaviour

Chin, Lili, *Doggie Language: A Dog Lover's Guide to Understanding Your Best Friend* (Summersdale, 2020)
Fogle, Bruce, *The Dog's Mind* (Michael Joseph, 1992)
Ha, James C. and Campion, Tracy L., *Dog Behavior: Modern Science and Our Canine Companions* (Academic Press, 2018)

### Nutrition

Boyd, Dr Jacqueline, *Canine Nutrition: Food, Feeding and Function* (Crowood Press, 2023)
Case, Linda P., *Dog Food Logic: Making Smart Decisions for Your Dog in An Age Of Too Many Choices* (Dogwise Publishing, 2014)
Habib, R. and Shaw Becker, Dr K., *The Forever Dog: A New Science Blueprint for Raising Healthy and Happy Canine Companions* (Harper Collins, 2021)

## Websites

www.k9trailtime.com
www.canicrosscoach.com
www.canicross.org.uk
www.thebssf.org.uk
www.canix.co.uk
www.canicross.international/en
www.sleddogsport.net

## Podcasts

https://podcasts.apple.com/gb/podcast/the-active-dog-podcast/id1616185764
https://podcasts.apple.com/gb/podcast/canicross-conversations/id1586295166

# Index

First published in 2025 by
The Crowood Press Ltd
Ramsbury, Marlborough
Wiltshire SN8 2HR

enquiries@crowood.com
www.crowood.com



British Library Cataloguing-in-Publication Data
A catalogue record for this book is available from the British Library.

ISBN 978 0 7198 4483 6

Cover design by Su Richards



Typeset by Simon and Sons
Printed and bound in India
by Parksons Graphics Pvt. Ltd.

## Acknowledgements

This book could not have been written without the help and support of so many friends, colleagues, clients and my family, in particular Marc, who puts up with my crazy lifestyle in order for me to pursue my goals.

I would like to thank the canicross community, who are my extended family, and have supported me since I started this sport.

To everyone at Crowood who gave me the confidence to share my book with the world, I am so grateful for the chance to fulfil a lifelong dream.

Thanks also to you, the reader; I hope this book helps you to understand the fantastic sport of canicross and gives you the connection with your dog that I have found with mine, through the shared activity of running.

Special thanks to the extremely talented Rae Prince, of Rae Prince Photography, who provided all the professional photographs in the book, except photos provided by myself or used with the consent of the following contributors: Harris Dickenson; Atlanta Tideswell; Erin Fidler; Claire Spencer; Becky Brown; Becky Harding, Hound and About Photography; Jo Minter; Mel Trevor.

## Dedication

This book is dedicated to my dogs, past, present and future, who have taught me so much, and changed my life for the better.